Single Mom Seeking

PLAYDATES, BLIND DATES

AND OTHER DISPATCHES FROM THE

DATING WORLD

Rachel Sarah

SEAL PRESS

SINGLE MOM SEEKING
Playdates, Blind Dates, and Other Dispatches from the Dating World
Copyright © 2006 Rachel Sarah

Published by
Seal Press
An Imprint of Avalon Publishing Group, Incorporated
1400 65th Street, Suite 250
Emeryville, CA 94608

AVALON
publishing group incorporated

ISBN-13: 978-1-58005-166-8 (alk. paper)
ISBN-10: 1-58005-166-9 (alk. paper)
9 8 7 6 5 4 3 2 1

Library of Congress Cataloging-in-Publication Data

Sarah, Rachel.
Single mom seeking : playdates, blind dates, and other dispatches from the dating world / Rachel Sarah.
p. cm.
Includes bibliographical references and index.
ISBN-13: 978-1-58005-166-8 (alk. paper)
ISBN-10: 1-58005-166-9 (alk. paper)
1. Single mothers. 2. Dating (Social customs) 3. Single mothers—Sexual behavior. I. Title.

HQ759.915.S152 2006
306.73086'9470973—dc22
 2006012048

Cover design by Gia Giasullo
Interior design by Tabitha Lahr
Back cover photo by © Johannah Hetherington
Printed in the United States of America by Malloy
Distributed by Publishers Group West

To Mae, my true love,
who has shown me in her own way *not* to settle

A Note from the Author

Names, dates, and identifying characteristics of many men portrayed in this book have been obscured for literary consistency, to protect privacy, and so none of the guys will send me hate mail.

Rachel Sarah
November 2006

Contents

Introduction 1

Chapter One: UPS Man at My Door 13

Chapter Two: Day 140:
My First Date as a Mom 31

Chapter Three: Who's Your Daddy? 60

Chapter Four: Coming Home 102

Chapter Five: Single Mom Seeking 125

Chapter Six: Red-Flag Alert 135

Chapter Seven:
Offline, and Back to Reality 156

Chapter Eight: JDate, Here I Come 179

Chapter Nine: Matchmaker, Matchmaker 204

Postscript: Where Are They Now? 218

Introduction

My life was *not* supposed to look like this.

I was supposed to be married to my soul mate by now, some strapping, easygoing, here's-a-love-note-in-your-pocket kind of fellow. He was supposed to be the kind of man who'd mix up a mean stir-fry on the stove and give me massages before bed. We were supposed to be the couple who winked at one another across the room at cocktail parties, the ones who knew how to argue—without fighting.

Ah, the hopes we have.

Who knew that my reality would turn out to be oh-so-different?

There's no make-believe about single parenting. It's you and only you in the middle of the night when your baby is crying. You are the sole comfort when your baby has an earache or fever. You are on your own when you need a shower and your baby is fussing in the bouncy seat on the tiled floor. Single parenting is my biggest life challenge thus far.

In 2003, I began writing a column "Single Mom Seeking" for the online magazine *Literary Mama* about how complex, messy, and draining single parenting can be. I got an astonishing response. Many single moms wrote me to say they were relieved that they weren't the only ones because, as one mom wrote, "single motherhood is hard to get your arms around, forget about trying not to feel like a failure when your house is a disaster." Subjects I addressed in my columns ranged from giving my very-involved dad a "time-out" to telling my daughter about condoms after she found one in the bathroom.

Yes, I was a woman *and* a mother—always trying to be on the ball, but often feeling like the balls were coming down on my head. But how was I going to add dating to my already jam-packed life? Don't get me wrong: When I landed a gig with a San Francisco newspaper as a monthly romance columnist, I was *not* in desperate pursuit of a man. The Man was not the key to my happiness. Although, in my weaker moments, I thought that maybe he was.

Life was about finding a balance between being a parent and a lover. Was there such a thing? I didn't know. But I was as sure as the countless nights my daughter wanted mac and cheese for dinner that I would find out. Many dates and red flags later, I emerged from it all with a much more realistic sense of who I am and what I want.

As I wrote this book, I hoped I would find a man along the way. Was I often discouraged? Bitching to my girlfriends and to anyone who would listen? Given to bouts of cynicism when I felt I would only see red flags and never a green light? Most definitely, yes. But I was still optimistic. What I've learned is no matter how a date ends, what really matters at the end of the day is coming home to my girl-power house and kissing my first love, my daughter.

This book covers my five years and counting of motherhood and dating, starting in New York City in 2000, when I found myself the suddenly single mom of a seven-month-old. Oh, those entertaining details of my first blind date when I quickly learned just how complex parenting and dating can be. Soon, I found myself with Boyfriend No. 1, the first "trial dad" in our lives. He and I didn't last, but boy-oh-boy, I was developing by leaps and bounds as a one-parent family—right alongside my daughter, who was growing and maturing every day.

Here I am today, at age thirty-three, living in the San Francisco Bay Area with my six-year-old daughter.

Where's that shy, stubborn girl from the Northern California suburbs who got straight As? Where's the young woman who was going to have a career before she had kids?

I was *not* supposed to be a single mom. I was supposed to start a family at the magic age of thirty-six, after I had a PhD in English literature framed on my office wall and a shimmering wedding ring on my left hand. Thirty-six. That's always been my favorite number. I was supposed to be a mom after meeting my future husband at the same university where I would be a tenured professor. We'd buy a house in a hip, liberal town like Berkeley and live in a sweet three-bedroom bungalow with a wild garden out back. As my belly grew, my partner and I would plant a tree for our baby-to-be, and after she arrived, we'd take her for dips in our hot tub out back. I was going to have a real family with a mama, a papa, and a baby.

In my dreams, right?

That first year as a single mom, at age twenty-eight, I clung to my baby girl as if she were my security blanket instead of the other way around. Domestic overdrive suited me fine: playing peekaboo, mopping the kitchen floor, dishing up kid-friendly food, changing diapers—and trying to get over my ex. My life orbited around my baby. Stacking blocks and reading board books with my daughter were my weekend highlights. I scheduled my work timetable around nursing her, getting her to nap, and pushing her on the swings. I also walked around with my head down, afraid to look a man in the eye, lest our eyes lock and I get swept away again. What I really wanted was someone to feed me, read me a bedtime story, pick me up off the floor, and give me a well-deserved piggyback ride.

But when I lifted my head two years later, I no longer wanted to shut out the possibility of dating, and sex.

Little did I know what weaning would do to my daughter, let alone to me. My cuddly, breastfeeding little babe was now an energetic two-year-old who kissed with a speedy peck on the cheek. She no longer wanted to lie in my arms. She was walking now—literally walking away from me to play with her friends. Her naps were a thing of the past.

As for me, I was certain that I'd lost all sensitivity in my nipples. Not so. My round abundant breasts were sagging now. But, boy, they were tingling again, and something was definitely stirring deep down inside.

Yes, a switch had been flipped inside this single mom—my libido was back. And so was my need to find a mate.

I decided to leave New York, where I'd been living for six years, and move to Berkeley, where my daughter and I had a support team of friends and family.

That summer, online dating was the talk of the town. *It's so-not-me*, I thought. I'm the kind of woman who has to see a man in the flesh to fall in love. Computers are for word processing, *not* man hunting. (As my single mom friend Siobhan puts it, "I have to smell a man! You can't do that on a computer screen!")

I met plenty of men, but they—tucked behind the counter of Ace Hardware or Whole Foods. Their distance felt safe, and I wasn't ready for anything serious. Safe, no-strings sex was easy enough to find. Having a relationship was the tough part.

Despite my longing for a man in my bed—and okay, sometimes sheer horniness—I really wanted a lifelong companion, a partner-in-parenting, a man who'd come bed with me for the rest of my life.

My first summer in Berkeley, I saw a flyer posted for a group called "Writing About Motherhood," facilitated by a local professor and mom, Amy Hudock, for mothers to come together with their kids and write. Minus little scratches in my journal, I hadn't written anything personal for a couple of years. The group eventually developed into *Literary Mama*, the online literary magazine featuring writing about motherhood. In creating my column, "Single Mom Seeking," I originally thought that if I could make sense of my life as a single mom on the page, maybe I could bargain a man into the deal somehow. I didn't expect the flood of responses I got from other single moms seeking:

I was so happy to read some of your stories . . . my husband walked out on my daughter and me on the day I was in the hospital having an emergency C-section. . . . Articles on single parenting are scarce. So reading your story particularly helped, because it made me realize that I am not alone.

I'm glad to know that I'm not the only one. . . . Thank you for sharing; I felt as though I could have written it myself.

You are the first woman I ever met who is like me! I was starting to think I was some kind of anomaly.

Writing my column made me realize I didn't have it so bad. I liked calling the shots. I liked giving my little girl one-on-one attention. After her bedtime, I liked having my own space to simply sit with myself. I'm no parenting expert. I simply wrote from the trenches.

Still, I missed having a man. When I decided to date again, I learned just how thorny that mix—parenting and dating simultaneously—can be. It's challenging to schedule weekly playdates for your child; add weekly blind dates to your agenda, and things can get chaotic. It's tough enough negotiating issues such as sleeping with a man for the first time—not to mention birth control. Now, throw in a kid and parenting concerns and responsibilities, and it gets really interesting. Inviting a man home after a date is one thing, but doing so when your child is sleeping in the next room becomes something else entirely.

Part of what I've learned as a romance columnist and a serial dater is how important it is to have a dating plan. I'm not talking about a long list of qualifications that your husband-to-be must meet. I'm talking about your own personal plan to scout for men consciously. This means knowing at the end of a first date, "I'll pass on this guy." This means saying "no" to a man with addictions and weird intentions. This means asking a man questions before inviting him to bed.

It's not easy to meet men when you're a single parent. You get easily sidetracked by the bills, mealtime, grocery shopping, carpooling, rent. And, yes, by your child, too.

But I wrote this book to say that you *can* date in between changing diapers and flipping the Raffi tape to side two. (I fell in love for the first time post-baby with a man who came to meet me at our local playground. He showed up on our first real date while I was nursing my daughter, with my blouse unbuttoned and both breasts hanging out.)

I wrote this book because it helped me figure out exactly what I want in life, and how to go about getting it. I wrote this book to stay sane while dating as a single parent. I wrote this book because it helped pull me out of my dating pitfalls.

And, to be honest, I wrote this book to find my own Mr. Right.

For the first two years back on the dating scene, I ignored the hype of online dating and met men in other ways. I flirted with cute men who worked in stores. Friends set me up. I didn't get lucky in love. But meanwhile I gained a tight tribe of other men who have been there for my daughter and me. These are really great men we can always count on—my dad, my stepdad, a sweet male neighbor, and the fathers of my daughter's friends.

When I turned thirty-one, my girlfriends dared me to post my profile on Match.com, the online dating service. They didn't really expect me to find my life partner in the aisles of the local Whole Foods. They also knew that I had a history of meeting someone and falling hard for them. I'd never really learned how to date. It was about time I learned how to screen men and ask questions first. I had to learn to trust my instincts, to recognize a red flag, to know a dealbreaker when I saw one.

I've always been the kind of woman who jumps at a dare, and new adventures have always thrilled me—especially when they involve a man. So, online I went.

"Are you an honest, big-hearted man with no addictions, except coffee?" I asked in the first line of my Match.com profile.

I organized all "my men" in a thick, three-ringed binder. Gary, the divorced businessman, liked watching movies that make him sad. Robby looked like a Calvin Klein ad and went to AA meetings every week to stay sober. Ronaldo, the father of two, was completing his PhD in psychology at UC Berkeley.

A funny thing happens when you decide to open yourself up to a new possibility like dating. It actually happens. I went on Match.com dates, blind dates, set-up dates, and, finally, JDates. I went on one or two dates a week, thanks to my girlfriends and my family who took my daughter on those evenings. But again, I'm not only a romance columnist and a dater—I'm a single mom.

In 2005, I landed a gig as a monthly columnist for a San Francisco weekly newspaper, in which I "outed" myself as a single mom looking for a date. So much for sympathy from single moms. Now I had local single men writing to me, asking me out.

I read every single-parent how-to dating book out there. They instruct readers to meet their dates in public places and not get too serious too soon. I broke every rule in those books. I've never been good at keeping boundaries with men. I've skipped the friendship chapter and jumped right into the romance. I've flirted with men in kid-friendly places like the playground or a school carnival. I've introduced my daughter way too early in relationships because I selfishly wanted to show her off: "She's something else, isn't she?" I've impulsively invited men over for the night, shooing my sister out of my apartment as I thanked her for babysitting Mae and putting her to bed, and then shooing the guy out the door at daybreak.

I took a lot of comfort from writer Anne Lamott who wrote in *Operating Instructions: A Journal of My Son's First Year*, "Sometimes I'm so hungry for a partner, a lover. One thing I know for sure, though, is that when you are hungry, it is an act of wisdom each time you turn down a spoonful if you know that the food is poisoned."

Operating Instructions, however, came out in 1993, around the time that our former vice president Dan Quayle attacked *Murphy Brown*, the sitcom, for featuring a lead character who decides to become a single mom. Quayle's distress about the absence of the father and his scapegoating of the single mother still happen more than a decade later—although the stigma isn't so potent.

When I started writing details of my sex life in my *Literary Mama* column, my married-mother friends worried about my personal safety and vulnerability. I got caught by my daughter at daybreak as I lay naked in bed with a man who was, well, exposed. And I watched my first-date skirt fray at the seams from too much wear.

I also met some really nice men, the kind of men who push my daughter high on the swings, let her win at Chutes and Ladders, and read her Dr. Seuss. None of these men will become my future husband, but each showered my daughter with gifts:

coloring books, markers, Sleepytime Herb Tea, and sparkly, rainbow-colored Band-Aids.

But I wanted to meet a nice man who also made my heart sing, a man who saw my single-mom status as an asset—or at least not a problem or liability.

And this is actually the case—at least in Hollywood, where single motherhood has become hip. Ariel Gore, author of *The Mother Trip: Hip Mama's Guide to Staying Sane in the Chaos of Motherhood,* credits hot single moms like Angelina Jolie for taking some of the shame out of single motherhood. She writes, "They're putting other family structures out there, and it helps people's grandmas be like, 'Well, I guess that's how they're doing things these days.'"

A recent headline in *Us Weekly* announces "The New Single Moms and How They Do It." The magazine spotlights Camryn Manheim's "new life as a single mother" shortly following the birth of her son, and also provides brief bios on Jodie Foster, Calista Flockhart, Diane Keaton, Rosie O'Donnell, Katie Couric, and Nicole Kidman. The article proclaims, quoting Aretha Franklin, that in Hollywood, "sisters are doing it for themselves."

Yes, single motherhood has come a long way since the 1977 movie *The Goodbye Girl,* about a divorced mother and her daughter who are forced to move in with an off-off-Broadway actor. Single motherhood has come even further since the stigma of *Murphy Brown.* In 2005, for instance, we saw *The Perfect Man,* with Hilary Duff playing the daughter of a single mom who tries to find, well, the perfect man for her mother. The final product is a sappy, yet thoughtful, tribute to single mothers.

One thing that will never go out of style is the importance of having a tribe, especially for a single mom who's the all-in-one parent. Being a single mom made me realize how much community matters. My best friends, Siobhan and Arden, are single moms, too, both with daughters. For the past three years, we've met every Tuesday after work at one of our East Bay apartments for a potluck dinner. Arden's four-year-old daughter named our evenings Girls Night Out. Each week, one of us makes the main dish, while the others bring veggies and salads. We fill each other in about parental anxieties, work stress, and menstrual schedules. We tell each other about screaming at our girls in public and losing our house keys who knows where.

"Please absolve me," one of us usually says.

We always do.

These women know that being a single mom isn't easy or graceful. They've helped me erase the shame by reminding me that it's great to be the one who calls all the shots, that our girls are thriving with all the exclusive attention they get from us.

"I can't go through with this," I've told Siobhan and Arden before meeting a new man. (Without fail, I always got the jitters before a blind date.)

"You're ravishing," Siobhan always would say. "Just look at you!"

"You're the ultimate catch," Arden would add. "Both you and Mae!"

On our most recent Girls Night Out, we asked Arden just how in love she is with her boyfriend of six months. (We adore him. After all, he *is* giving her up to us once a week.) We asked Siobhan how she's doing *sans* boyfriend. (As usual, she is perfectly happy this way.)

None of us is on a frantic hunt for a husband. Well, this is a slight contradiction, I admit. Our future dreams do include a life partner.

Whenever I planned a date, I scheduled a playdate for my daughter, too. If I had a weekend date, my dad took her to the Oakland Zoo or a kids' matinee. If I had an overnight date, a friend or a family at her preschool jumped at the chance to have Mae for a slumber party. Mostly, Mae and I stayed as close as ever. We had plenty of mother-daughter time, strolling through Fairyland to catch a puppet show, building sand castles at Lake Anza, picking fresh mint from our garden, painting with acrylics in the kitchen.

I'm going on Year Six of Single Motherhood.

It's not easy crossing over from Mom to Single Mom Seeking. A mother is nurturing, soft, and sometimes frumpy. A mother doesn't wear tight skirts and black boots. She doesn't have one-night stands or flirt with random men while grocery shopping. She most emphatically does not own a first-date skirt.

With all the dating I've been doing lately, you'd think I'd be good at making the transition between domestic and nurturing Mom to sexy and available Single. But it's not easy crossing over.

Some days still suck.

When I tell Arden about my upcoming date, and how exhausted I am, she says, "Well, you need more material for your book, don't you?"

"No," I say, defensively. "I'm serious about meeting someone. I have plenty of material already."

I've been so worn out that I've screamed at my daughter on the street corner and then left our house keys in the front door all night. I've made silent prayers that my life will magically turn out the way Madonna's and Angelina Jolie's did—making single motherhood look so chic and easy, and then hooking up with the men of their dreams.

When I picked my daughter up from kindergarten recently, she confessed, "I have a crush on Becky," a new friend of hers. Then she ordered me to wash her pink and gray pants from Old Navy because Becky has the identical jacket and they want to match tomorrow.

These are the moments I wish I could share with her father. Together we could watch as she shows us how she can hula hoop for five minutes straight, finger knit, draw a horse, and turn somersaults in the swimming pool.

But every time I turn around, I'm pleasantly surprised to see that even without a dad around, my daughter is doing just fine. She's a poised and composed little girl whom her teacher describes as "a sought-after playmate . . . an absolute joy to have in class."

And me? I'm still the same free-spirited adventuress I always was. But my pace is more deliberate now, as I balance on the stepping-stones of life, instead of running in circles on the track. Motherhood has changed me. I am first and foremost a mom, dedicated completely to my daughter's well-being. Mae Frances Anne will always come first.

Chapter One:
UPS Man at My Door

My very first single-motherhood crush is on the UPS man.

It's the winter of 2001, and I've been a single mom for barely two months when my baby girl and I move into a new apartment in Washington Heights. Clutching nine-month-old Mae on my hip, I squeeze into the elevator with the UPS man and his massive rolling cart. I am just inches away from his tight muscular arms.

"Hi!" Mae says, waving her hand at him. She has recently started to say hi to anyone.

"Hi!" she tries again.

"Oh, hi, beautiful!" the UPS man says, reaching out and touching her knee.

His sleeve is rolled up on his forearm, and I steal a glance at his muscles.

"It's gonna be another late night over here," he says. I'm amazed that he's talking to me.

"Oh yeah?" I say.

"Just work, work, work."

"Don't you ever play?" I say, flirtatiously, and my cheeks turn red. He looks into my eyes. "I bowl on Friday nights and have my daughter on Sundays."

"You have a daughter?"

"She just turned eight. Her mama and I separated last year, so I get her two days a week."

"I'm sorry to hear that," I say.

But I'm not sorry at all. No, I'm not sorry one tiny bit.

When the door opens on the fourth floor, no one moves.

"Excuse me, isn't this you?" he asks.

"Oh!" I wake up, realizing that, yes, we *do* live on the fourth floor. As I step off the elevator, I realize that he knows where we live. Does that mean he has actually noticed me before?

My face is burning hot as I walk down the long corridor to our apartment. I am thinking of the two of us stuck inside the elevator one afternoon, with the doors shut and no way to get out. No one pushes the EMERGENCY button. No one screams for help. He steps toward me and kisses my forehead. I reach out and touch his chest, just above his top button, where it's moist from a good day's work.

"*Mmmm,*" he says, as he gently squeezes my nipple through my shirt.

I am still thinking about him when I walk into the apartment. I sit on the sofa and nurse Mae, and meander through another daydream: It's a sun-drenched day, and I'm pushing my daughter in the stroller; she falls asleep without a fuss, just as the big UPS truck pulls up, and the UPS man hops out. He tells me that he's going on a break, and asks if I want to go on a walk. We stroll along the Hudson River, talking about our daughters. Our hands accidentally touch. That's when he leads me over to the stone wall where there's a view of the river and, without a word, he kisses me. His lips taste like mango. I want more. He reaches around and cups my ass. I lean into him, pressing my chest against his. He gently nibbles on my bottom lip. I have to hold my breath to keep from moaning in bliss.

On the sofa, Mae pulls off my breast and milk squirts on to the pillow. She laughs. My fantasy is now over. Back to reality.

You've lost it, I think. *You're nursing your daughter and having a mental make-out session with the UPS man.*

But the truth is, I am longing for some affection.

My daughter satisfies all my maternal needs; I love her unconditionally. But who is satisfying my need for companionship and, let's face it, for intimacy? It's no secret that being with a partner makes me less anxious, more confident, and just plain happy.

So, where is he?

Having a relationship with the UPS man could be the perfect solution to my present loneliness. Dating right now seems too daunting. But how convenient would it be to have this man arrive on my doorstep, the goods delivered as promised?

If only it were that easy: a knock at the door and I open it to find this gorgeous hunk standing there in his brown uniform. I never have to leave my apartment; he simply shows up.

That evening, as Mae and I are walking back from the drugstore, I can barely look at all the couples out for an evening walk without feeling jealous. Those women have access to safe and loving sex with men who adore them. Though in reality I'm sure they have their problems, in my fantasy they have ideal relationships. And I want that too, dammit.

The next day at the playground, I overhear two moms chatting:

Mom No. 1: *He's always ready to pounce on me, right at bedtime. I'm tired!*

Mom No. 2: *Tell me about it. The last thing on my mind at night is doing it.*

Mom No. 1: *To tell the truth, I could take it or leave it—*

Mom No. 2: *Yeah, sleep is a lot more precious than sex.*

I stand there, feeling like a voyeur. Do they realize how good they have it? What I would do right now to have a man welcome me with open arms into bed every night.

⬚▰⬚▰

A month earlier, I try to pull open the heavy metal door at 690 Fort Washington Avenue—but it won't budge.

"Mama's got it, sweetie," I tell my baby, as she squirms on my hip.

I do this often—reassure Mae that I have everything under control—because I want her to believe it, even if I don't.

I am here to sign a lease for a small one-bedroom apartment in Washington Heights because it's impossible for me to live in my current apartment, heartbroken, with too many memories of Mae's father, Eric. I also need a smaller, more affordable place. The rooms in our apartment snake around in one long line, and now that Mae is crawling, I can't manage to keep my eyes on her. I'll be making dinner in the kitchen and turn around to find her scooting away from her stack of blocks. I drop my spoon and give chase as she crawls into the next room.

A panicky first-time mom, I worry that she'll burn herself on the radiator or bump her head on the corner of a table. But I also need a new start: A smaller place in a new building away from the memory of Eric seems like it will solve both problems.

I am ten minutes late to meet Raul, the building manager. Maybe I am supposed to push this door, not pull it. I try, but it's no use. When I peer through the window, I can see the manager waiting for me in the lobby.

I wave. Doesn't he see me? I try pushing again, putting my whole body—and Mae's—into it this time. I feel like a fool: Why can't I even open a goddamn door? I want to close the doors to my past, so I can open new ones, but I can't even deal with the one right in front of me.

Umph! I groan, leaning hard against the door.

Just then, the manager jumps up and pulls the handle. I almost fall on him.

"I'm so sorry," I say.

Raul is slight; at five feet two, he's only a couple of inches taller than I am. He has wavy dark hair, brown eyes, and a soft voice. When he walks alongside me, I feel like everything is going to work out. He seems like a nice guy.

"Your daughter is beautiful," Raul says in the elevator as we ride up to the fourth floor.

"Thanks," I say.

"Man!" Mae blurts out, pointing at Raul, as if he is some rare species.

Yes, sweetheart, I think, *we sure don't see many men these days.*

Raul unlocks the apartment door, and I follow him. "Just the two of you are moving in?" he asks, his voice curious.

"Yes," I say. "I'm a . . . I'm a . . ." I just can't say, "I'm a single mom." The words will not come out. That one simple sentence is trapped in so much fear, deep in my throat, like a bug with broken wings; there is no way it's going to fly out.

I take a breath and try again. "It's just the two of us."

Raul nods sympathetically, and hands me a pen and a stack of papers to sign. Just as I bend over the first page, Mae grabs the pen out of my hand.

"Mommy needs that right now," I say, as she bites on the end of it.

"I'm really sorry," I say to Raul, who seems amused. "She's teething."

I pull a cracker out of my bag and offer Mae a trade: She accepts. I sign the first page; there are at least ten more to read through. But Mae has already swallowed the cracker and is wiggling on my hip.

Raul starts making puckering sounds, trying to distract her. *Pop! Pop!* This isn't working. Mae is twisting so much that each signature gets sloppier.

"Can I hold her?" Raul asks. Without thinking, I hand her over to him. She goes easily, right into his arms.

He coos to her, his muscular arms softly holding her; then he tosses her in the air, and she giggles. When I glance up from my paper, Raul is looking at me. I look back at the lease, pretending to read every word.

I am so far removed from any possibility of romance that I don't realize that maybe, just maybe, he is checking me and my little family out.

Tonight, in our new apartment, I bring nine-month-old Mae into the bathroom to get ready for bed. When you're a single parent who's about to hit the sack, you don't exactly primp and fuss over yourself. Why bother when you're just snuggling up with a wiggly munchkin in diapers who is going to pull your hair and drool on you? When I was with Eric, getting ready for bed meant brushing out my long brown hair, spraying a bit of rose water on my neck, and swishing around some mouthwash.

Mmmm, baby here I come.

Nowadays, I snuggle with another kind of baby.

When I bend over Mae to change her diaper—I use only cloth during the day, but plastic at night—I sing, "Twinkle, twinkle, little star . . ." She blows spit bubbles, reaching out with her little cinnamon toes to touch my cheeks, and I want to stay in this moment, loving her completely. I wash her face with a warm washcloth, put a clean onesie on her, and brush her teeth. Well, she doesn't exactly have teeth; I put a puppet-shaped plastic thing over my index finger and rub it over her gums. I brush my teeth, too, and feel the throb of a cavity in the back. I've been ignoring it for months. I haven't been to the dentist for more than a year.

I'm twenty-eight years old, deemed a young mom by most New Yorkers. Moreover, I simply *look* young. I break out. I blush easily. I have freckles. Strangers often ask me what I'm studying in school. No, I'm not your picture of a single mom by choice, not one of those forty-something career women who hear their biological clock ticking and decide to raise a child on their own.

More than a handful of times, strangers on the subway have asked me, "Is it hard being a teen mom?" I turn my head to look over my shoulder, before I realize they're talking to *me*.

As I sit down on the toilet to pee, Mae dumps a box of hair clips on the tiled floor. As I bend down to pick them up, I look down at the toilet paper and see reddish brown.

What the—? I think. What's wrong with me?

It's been so long since I've had my period—eighteen months to be exact—that my blood catches me off guard. I haven't missed getting my period. It's unexpected right now.

My blood looks old and rusty, not bright and new. Getting my period means, of course, that I can get pregnant again. My body is still producing eggs. My mother always warned me about my Irish roots: "The women in our family are very, very fertile." And it was startling how easily I'd conceived. The first time I had unprotected sex with Eric, we made Mae.

But at this moment, the last thing I want is another baby. I have no tampons, so I roll up a bunch of toilet paper and put it in my underwear.

"We're going on a walk," I tell Mae.

I tuck her into the sling. "We're going to the pharmacy," I say to her, as if I'm talking to an adult, as if my nine-month-old understands my every word. I have to stop it. But it's what being a single parent will do to you.

I pull a cotton cap over Mae's head—she has a soft tuft of light brown hair now—and we're off. The sun is setting, and there's a nip in the air; we've had our last winter snow, but spring hasn't arrived yet.

Right there on our corner, my UPS man is pushing a huge box on a handcart, coming toward us in his customary brown shirt and slacks.

Eavesdropping recently on a conversation he was having with another tenant, I found out his name is Otis. As I walk toward him, I check out his smooth, shaved head and solid arms.

"Out for an evening walk?" he asks in his deep New York accent.

"Yeah," I say, squeezing my legs together and hoping that nothing is seeping through my pants.

But I'm more worried that he'll figure out I have a crush on him. I wouldn't even know how to begin a new relationship. I'm such an emotional mess, rooted only by the day-to-day care of my baby. What if something flirtatious slips out of my mouth, and I offend him? What if he actually likes me, and I really fall for him, and then slowly, all my faults leak out? At this point, any kind of future with any man is unimaginable.

I remind myself that a crush is just harmless fun.

"You're not cold?" Otis says with a smile.

My arms are bare, the hair rising on them. I was so concerned about bundling up Mae that I forgot to dress myself in something warm.

"I'm okay," I say, lying.

I'm self-conscious; I want to hurry down the street and get my damn tampons. Up to this point, we've hardly exchanged a "hi" in the building lobby. Why does he have to initiate a conversation right now?

"You're working late tonight?" I ask, trying to be polite.

"I usually do," he says, winking at me. "I've just got to keep going until I've delivered everything."

Here is a man who delivers. He's so responsible, so accountable. He's everything Mae's father is not.

"Well, good luck," I say. I feel ridiculous as I walk backward down the sidewalk, in case there's a giant red spot on my butt.

When we get to the store, my daughter screams, "Mae!"

She points to the orange tabby cat that lives here. She and the cat have the same name. Mae kicks in my arms, wanting to get down and follow the cat. But I've been warned this cat is so aggressive even the neighborhood dogs fear her.

Mae kicks so hard that her shoes crash into my belly. I pull her out of the sling and put her down, letting her crawl on the (relatively) clean carpet toward the tampon aisle at the other end of the store.

But Mae wants to go the other way. "No!"

"Honey, this way," I say, although what I really want to tell her is, "Your mommy's bleeding. C'mon!"

I know better than to incite a tantrum. "The kitty's over here," I say, pointing toward the tampon aisle.

But she can see that the cat is right in front of her. Tricking this smart gal is not going to work tonight. I bend down and try to pick her up, but she twists away from me.

"No!" she shrieks again.

"Mae! We're going this way!" I say, sounding just like those bossy mothers in the store who make me cringe, the ones I swear I'll never be like.

I go one way, and she crawls the other. This is just the start of our mother-daughter struggle. Mae is not even a year old, and already we're clashing. "Come here!" I say again, but she ignores me, dropping to her belly and scooching under a table displaying organic makeup. She heads right toward the cat.

Part of me wants to just leave her there for a minute, grab a box of tampons—and maybe a box of anesthetizing drugs from the medicine aisle—and come right back. But at that moment, Mae juts her hand out to the cat, who mistakes her for a giant predator and lashes out, scratching her hand.

"*Waaaaaaaaaaahhh!*" Mae cries.

When I pick her up, blood is dripping from her pinky finger. I cradle her in my arms, but she's still wailing.

A store employee comes over. "Excuse me. Is everything okay?"

"The cat scratched her," I say, feeling like I'm going to break down and cry myself.

"Let me see," the woman says, reaching for Mae's hand. But Mae jerks her hand back and tucks it into her chest; blood drips on her jacket.

Something wet leaks between my legs. We've got to get out of here. This is unjust: All I need is a tampon. If I had a man at home—a husband, a real partner—I could leave my baby with him for ten minutes, run down to the store, buy a box of tampons, and get back home in a jiffy.

Ten minutes and one Band-Aid later, we're out the door. That's when I start talking to myself. *Let's face it, Rachel. From here on out, it's just you and your baby. This is your life now. Wherever you go, she goes, and that's that.*

Mae holds her finger to her chest, whimpering. The walk back to our apartment is long and cold.

A week after my period ends, I'm thinking about how long it's been. As in, how long it's been since I was with a man. No man has touched me since Eric left. *Not one.*

I've heard that if babies aren't touched, they won't develop normally; certain connections in their brain actually disappear. How about women? What happens when we're not touched?

When I nurse Mae, I get that rush of oxytocin. It always catches me off guard. As my milk comes down, heat rushes through my chest, down to my pelvis, and I stiffen up. I don't want to depend on my baby to satisfy my physical need to be touched. That's not *right*. I should be feeling this with a man, not my baby girl.

Pre-baby, I loved to flirt. I wore tight clothes. I showed some skin. I went out with my coworkers for a beer and smoked an occasional cigarette. Who would I take home with me tonight? I once shared an office with a very cute editor at a small publishing house in the West Village. We used to meet on the fire escape at lunch and kiss for half an hour, and then go back to editing elementary school textbooks with smiles on our faces. It thrilled me to go against workplace rules. When he put his arms around me, I relaxed. His lips on mine were like licking cake batter off my finger.

Chatting with a man used to be easy. Now I don't have a clue. My days are occupied by nursing my baby, burping her, rocking her to sleep. I'm on the job 24/7. In the kitchen, I mash her baby food, wipe it off the floor, and wash out her plastic bowls and spoons. I go everywhere in sweatpants and T-shirts stained with spit-up. I shower infrequently and haven't had my hair cut since Mae was born.

Every night, I gently wrap one arm around my little girl in bed, and wish I had another arm—a man's—wrapped around both of us. Mae will not remember sleeping in between her parents, like a warm hot dog tucked into a bun.

When we're out, I sense that strangers are trying to figure us out. At the playground, I'm often mistaken for being Mae's baby sitter. "How long have you been with her?" I'm asked.

"Since birth," I say, with a smirk on my face.

Mae and I don't look alike: I'm white, of Irish and Polish descent; Eric is African American, with a bit of American Indian.

Mae has dark curls, cinnamon skin, and full lips. My eyes are blue, hers are grayish green. Many people assume we're not related.

After people realize we're related, I often have this conversation:

Stranger: *She's gorgeous! She must be quite the daddy's girl.*
Me: *Actually, the dad's not in the picture.*
Stranger: *Not in the picture? Are you divorced?*
Me: *No, he walked out on us.*
Stranger: *Oh, I'm sorry. Maybe he'll be back . . .*
Me: *No, it's been six months, and there hasn't been any sign of him.*

I've told this story to nameless strangers, all the details slipping out of me. My psyche is desperate to talk about it, to make sense of what happened, and move on.

My doorbell rings and I push the TALK button on the intercom.

"Who is it?"

"UPS."

I forgot all about ordering a used copy of Anne Lamott's *Operating Instructions: A Journal of My Son's First Year* as a ploy to see my UPS man as soon as possible. But here I am running around in circles, trying to straighten up a bit.

I am wearing a stretched-out tank top, Levi's cutoffs, and no makeup—not exactly what I had hoped to be wearing when I saw Otis again. I quickly pull the rubber band out of my hair, let it down over my shoulders, and open the door.

"Gosh, it's hot!" Otis says, extending his arm to give me the signature pad.

"It sure is!" I agree, as my cheeks flush.

"I've lost count of how many water bottles I downed today."

I wonder if he is dropping a hint, and I jump on it: "Are you thirsty? Would you like some lemonade?"

"Oh, no thank you," he says politely, handing over my package.

"It's really no trouble," I push. "I have some cold lemonade right here."

It just so happens that I have a carton of Newman's Own lemonade in the fridge.

"Well, why not?" he says, taking a step forward.

"Are you allowed to come in?" I whisper.

"Not really," he whispers back. "But as long as the boss doesn't see."

He takes one large stride into my apartment, and I quickly shut the door. There's a mass of unfolded laundry on the floor. A bag of stinky garbage leans against the wall, waiting for somebody to throw it out. Mae is naked, perched on top of our coffee table, watching *Sesame Street*. She's oblivious to our gorgeous male guest. If we had a sofa, I'd ask him to sit down. He'd probably break the table if he rested his brawny body on it, so I leave him by the door.

"Just wait there!" I say.

I drop the brown package on the coffee table next to Mae and rush to the kitchen. I hope he doesn't follow because it is one big, sticky mess back there, with dirty dishes crowding the kitchen sink. The linoleum floor is spotted with applesauce and sweet potato.

My fingers shake as I search the cupboard for a clean glass. I feel very naughty but pleased. Maybe he is my special delivery, my parcel of love. Maybe it is this simple; just open the door and find my bundle standing there.

Uh, maybe not.

A minute later, I'm back. And hopeful.

"Cold lemonade," I say, offering him the glass.

"Thanks," he says.

I watch him tip the lemonade to his lips. The ice cubes clink together.

My soul is singing: *The UPS man is inside my house, the UPS man is inside my house.*

He clutches his signature board with one hand and his glass with the other. I'd be content to stay here forever, next to this good-looking hunk of a man, listening to him gulp my lemonade.

A bead of sweat falls down his bald head, past his right ear, a big careless drop. I want to reach out and wipe it off. But he beats me to it.

Nobody says a word. And then the lemonade is gone.

Oh no, this is way too fast.

"Would you like some more?" I ask.

"No thanks," he says. "That really hit the spot." He hands the empty glass back to me.

I notice his forearm, how tight his muscle is right between his wrist and elbow. I want to bend over and kiss him right there. I think about what I'll do after he's gone, how I'll refill this glass with lemonade and drink it all alone. I'll sip from this glass, *his* glass, and imagine that I taste him.

I must be losing it. But it's been a long time.

"Mama!" Mae says from the living room.

I turn my head. "Yes?"

"Milk!" she says, pulling me back from my fantasy and into reality.

"Elmo's World" is over, and so is my opportunity to flirt. Otis hasn't even been here three minutes. Why can't I move faster? Why can't I get the ball rolling?

"I guess she's thirsty, too?" Otis says.

"Yeah," I say. I'm embarrassed—little does he know that when Mae says "milk," it actually means she wants to nurse. She has never been a baby who says *noo noo* or *na na*, but just plain "milk."

My daughter is a very articulate, straightforward little girl; I should take some tips from her.

"You said that your daughter is eight?" I ask, trying to keep our connection. I don't want him to go, not yet.

"Yes, she'll be nine this summer," he says.

"When?"

"In July, just like me," he says.

"Oh, you're a Cancer?" I ask. "I am, too! I'm July 20. So, are you emotionally needy?"

He raises his eyebrows. "Well, I guess my ex would say so."

"And you always need to be reminded that you're loved, right?" I ask, not quite believing the kinds of questions coming out of my mouth.

He laughs. "Whoa, you're deep."

I blush. I'm so desperate to know him right now. I'm impatient and raring to go.

"Milk!" Mae calls out again, pulling herself down from the coffee table.

"I'll be right there, sweetie," I say to her, without turning my eyes away from Otis.

"Maybe we can get together with the girls sometime?" Otis asks.

I hold my breath. "I'd love that!" I say. "How about Sunday?"

It's Friday, I think to myself. *That's only two days away.*

"Okay," he says. "We can come after church."

The next couple of days, I'm lost in fantasyland. In between nursing Mae and editing textbooks after hours on my computer, I imagine how sweet and grown-up Otis's daughter will be. She'll bond immediatcly with Mae. All big girls love babies, right? I envision Otis's daughter leading Mae to the bookshelf, where she'll read Mae one book after another. Perfect.

Then I'll casually turn to Otis and ask, "Would you like to see our view?" (There's no real view, of course, just a tiny slice of the Hudson River you can barely see if you stand on your tiptoes at the bedroom window.) He'll follow me dutifully into the other room, and I'll shut the door. At the window, our embrace will be automatic. Our mouths will open wide, tasting each other. Our tongues will dance, as I prop myself against the wall and he leans over me. He'll unbutton my blouse and reach his hand in, teasing my nipples. I'll moan hungrily, and he'll remind me about the girls.

Shhhh, I'll say, giggling.

I'll kiss his neck, tasting his salty skin. I'll feel him grow hard against me. That's when I'll reach down and tuck my hand into his pants, taking his hard dick in my hands. It has been so long, and damn, this man feels good!

On Sunday, the doorbell rings at three o'clock sharp.

"Oh!" I say to nobody, as I try to pull the zipper up on my skirt.

Mae is on the floor, tugging at my leg. "Mamaaaaaa . . ."

"It's okay, honey," I say. She didn't get her afternoon nap today. She's cranky, to put it mildly.

I'm wearing one of my miniskirts from those old office days, a cream blouse that shows a bit of cleavage, and long turquoise earrings. Mae and I have matching red clips in our hair, and I've put lipstick on for the first time in months. I've put her in a cotton pink dress with ruffles, but she keeps reaching under the hem and undoing her Velcro diaper cover.

When I open the door, I'm relieved to see Otis and his daughter dressed up, too. They're both in their church clothes. He looks so different—even more handsome, if that's possible—in his white, button-down shirt and creased black slacks.

"Hi," he says, reaching out and patting my arm.

"Hi," his daughter, Alicia, says, sticking close to her daddy.

"Come in!" I wave my hand. "Are you hungry? Thirsty?"

I want to be the best hostess in the whole wide world. I want to please him. I want to show him what a good mom I am. I set out some juice and crackers on the coffee table, but there's no place to really sit down, except for the throw pillows on the hardwood floor.

"Uh, I guess I've got the yoga studio motif going here," I say. "Are you okay on the floor?"

"Sure!" Otis says, as he tries to sit cross-legged on a bumpy pillow, a look of pain crossing his face. "My knee has been acting up lately, but I'm fine."

"Your knee?"

"It's an old football injury," he says. "Since I'm always on my feet at work, it doesn't help."

He grimaces. I want to go right over and massage his knee.

"Milk!" Mae demands, as she crawls to my feet.

"Here's a cracker, sweetheart," I say, offering her a rice cake.

She smacks it out of my hand. "No!"

I pick it up from the floor. "Someone didn't get a nap today," I tell Otis.

Damn, why can't she just get with the program and see that we have a man here?!

Meanwhile, Otis's daughter has gone over to the bookshelf, where she sits quietly and reads.

"Did you enjoy the sermon this morning?" I ask Otis.

He looks at me strangely. "Oh, yeah," he says dismissively. "It is what it is. I go because it makes my mom happy."

I've been so removed from any kind of organized religion for so many years that I don't really know how to talk to someone who goes to church.

"So, what do you like to do when you're not working?" I try again.

"I'm in a bowling league every Friday night," he says.

"Great!" I say. I've bowled a couple of times in my life, mostly gutter balls.

Then Mae starts to cry. "Milk!"

"Okay, okay," I say, letting out a sigh. I sit down with my back against the wall and hike my blouse up. I want to do this discreetly, but it's impossible. Mae is tugging on my boob. My blouse is so tight there's no way to squeeze her head under it.

"Uh, just a second," I say, getting up to find a blanket in the bedroom. I could take her back there to nurse, but I don't want to leave Otis. He's only just arrived.

In the living room, I drape the blanket over Mae's head. She sucks loudly and pulls the blanket off, revealing my pale breast.

Otis looks away. I try covering her head again, but she yanks the blanket right off. Even worse, as Mae sucks my left breast, she reaches up and grabs the right one. Lately, she has gotten into this habit of taking a sip from my left breast, then the right, and back to the left. Mastermind that my girl is, she has figured out that switching back and forth makes my milk come down faster.

I try to move her hand away from my right breast, which she is now squeezing as if she's milking a cow. But she jerks it right back, underneath my bra. This is not quite the scenario I'd imagined when I thought about going bare-breasted for Otis.

"How you doing over there, baby?" Otis says to his daughter, purposefully gazing away from me and my chest as Mae sucks noisily. Yes, this is very awkward.

One hour later, Otis and his daughter are back at the door, pulling their coats on. I give him a quick hug, but it feels futile. Wouldn't you know it: Mae has fallen asleep, lying peacefully on a pillow. And here I am, on my own again.

Chapter Two: Day 140: My First Date as a Mom

"I want to meet someone," I say a week later to Susan and Jim, my neighbors up the street.

Slumped over on their sofa, I'm wearing a ratty T-shirt and sweatpants.

"I'm sorry if I sound so whiny," I say, as I tell them about my awkward first single-motherhood rendezvous with the UPS man. It was nowhere *close* to a date, and even under those circumstances, I couldn't handle myself properly. I don't know how to flirt anymore. I don't know how to *talk* to a man anymore.

"Don't worry, you'll meet someone," Susan says. "Just give it some time."

Susan and Jim are a wonderfully neurotic Jewish couple with a daughter who is six months older than Mae. They live in a high-rise a few blocks from our apartment. They often invite us for dinner, and I'm incredibly grateful to them for adopting us.

"Well, I'm not really ready for a real relationship," I say to Susan. "Just sex."

She explodes into laughter: "Well, let's not be vague here!"

I turn red. Did I really just say that? But I'm serious.

Susan's eyes light up, and I can see her planning my wedding.

She yells into the kitchen, "Hey, Jim, not all hope is lost! Rachel's going to get her tush back out there!"

I trust my friends. They've known me since Mae was a couple of months old and have remained my friends even after Eric left. I also know that Susan and Jim have my well-being—and Mae's—in mind.

I also love their company. They always make me laugh. They are both lawyers. Their phone is always ringing, as the Grateful Dead streams through the living room. I dream about someday having what they have: someone to sit down to dinner with every night, to talk politics with, and to snuggle with in bed. (A year later, Susan will confess to me that they haven't had sex for months. At this moment, though, I believe their lives are everything mine is not.)

How can I even think about being with another man when I haven't gotten over Eric? When Mae and I moved into our apartment, I took many things Eric had left behind, as if I couldn't part with him. I brought his carpentry tools with us; I thought, *I'm going to teach myself how to use a drill and handsaw someday.* I haven't touched them. I kept one of his T-shirts with sweat stains in the armpits. I'll never wear it, but sometimes at night I pull it out and hold it close to my face, breathing him in. I also have his Levi's overalls, which I wore until I was so pregnant they wouldn't fit over my middle anymore. They hang in my closet, as if they're waiting for him to come back.

In my desk drawer, there's a little black earmuff from an airplane headset, a memento of the day we met. I was a twenty-six-year-old editor at a publishing house. I freelanced as a reporter on the side and got permission to leave my job for two weeks to cover a UN conference in The Hague. As I boarded the plane to Amsterdam, I noticed a man who had been bumped from his seat. He was six feet tall, with a goatee and shaved head, and a sincere look in his eyes. It just so happened there was an empty seat next to me, so I confidently marched up to him and offered it. That's how I met Eric.

One of the first things I noticed about him was the smell of alcohol on his breath. To most women, that would be a red flag. But I have a rescue complex and think I can handle people, even help them, especially men. As my mother always put it: "Rachel, you go about picking up these wounded birds and try to mend their wings."

Sometimes I think she might be right. No, I know she's right. Damn her.

Crawling across Susan and Jim's hardwood floor, Mae looks intently into my eyes, and in a split second, I see a flash of Eric. They are both very focused people; I'm grateful she inherited his depth of attention. She grasps my leg and climbs into my lap, wanting to nurse. She always brings me back to the present, and I love that about her.

I'm not the only one around here who's changing, feeling like my motherhood role is getting a bit too tight these days. When I recently took Mae to the Central Park Carousel, I fastened the seat belt snugly around her waist, and then wrapped my arm around her. But she tried to wiggle away.

"Self!" she said.

"By yourself?" I asked, attempting to translate.

"Self!" she screamed, trying to pull her little waist away from my hand. She didn't want me to hold on to her. I let go, and the carousel started spinning; Mae gripped the pole with both hands, looking very proud of herself.

"So, what are you looking for?" Jim asks, as he tips the sushi plate toward me.

"It's pretty simple," I say, leaning toward Susan so Mae can't hear. "He has to be single and attractive—oh, disease- and drug-free, too."

"Sounds easy enough," Jim says, over Mae's sucking sounds.

"Oh, and he needs to respect my space," I say, as I pet the top of Mae's head. "I can't have some guy knocking at my door at any hour of the day, wanting some booty."

Jim raises his eyebrows at me. I blush again. I must sound like I'm custom-ordering a night of casual (but safe) sex. So what? It's what I want. I look down at my shirt, which is stained with soy sauce, and at my sock, which has a hole in it. I can't really be serious about this.

When Jim passes the plate to Susan, he says to her, "Mark?"

"Oh, no!" Susan says. "Don't do that to Rachel."

"Don't do what?" I ask.

"He smokes pot," says Susan, as her daughter climbs into her lap to nurse.

"Last I heard, he'd quit smoking because the office was doing a drug test," Jim says.

"I thought he had a girlfriend," Susan says.

"They just broke up," Jim replies.

I sit between them, chewing a piece of seaweed, my eyes going back and forth as they debate this mystery man. I'm touched that they are so eager to make me a match, but Susan's hesitation makes me uneasy.

"He's an emotional fuck-up!" Susan says, although the girls are right here.

I shake my head. This was a bad idea.

"What I mean is," Susan goes on, "I don't think he's mature enough for Rachel—"

"She didn't say anything about needing him to be in therapy," Jim says. "It's just physical."

Susan turns to me and looks serious. "He recently asked us if we know any cute single women," she says. "He's very cute, but he has major commitment problems."

"Sounds great!" I say. Noncommittal is just what I need.

"He'd be perfect for a one-night stand," Susan adds. "But you can't get attached—"

"No problem!" I say.

It's Friday night, and I'm taking a shower before my blind date with Mark. Not only is it my first date since Mae was born, but it's my first blind date ever. Jim and Susan set it up, thinking Mark, their coworker at legal aid, would make a good match for a night of carefree passion.

How bad could it be? I wonder. A lawyer who provides free legal services to the poor can't be all bad.

After a pleasant chat on the phone, we decide to meet for drinks. I'm grateful for the chance to have a private shower before our date. I close my eyes and let the water wash over my cheeks. I can't remember the last time I showered without my baby girl in clear sight; usually, she's with me in the tub, bubbles and all.

My heart is thumping hard. This is a big deal: going out on my first date as a single mom. He's a lawyer, I remind myself; at least we'll have an intelligent, interesting conversation. That's not hoping for too much, right?

I open my eyes to find a razor. I better shave my legs. It's almost time to go.

My best friend, Amanda, is in the living room; she's the only person I trust to watch Mae while I'm out on the town, or at least out for a drink. I can hear her reading *Goodnight Moon*, one of Mae's favorite books. I'm grateful to Amanda for making the hour-long trip from the East Village to Washington Heights to baby-sit.

I stand on the bath mat and look in the mirror at the stretch marks that cross my belly. No man except Eric has seen them.

I'd heard that rubbing cocoa butter on my stomach while I was pregnant would prevent them, but it's not true. Massaging my fingers across these lines that are a permanent part of me, I think how life began here in this belly.

I conceived Mae the night of my twenty-seventh birthday, after a rooftop party in the East Village with Amanda and a few friends. I was beaming that night, so in love with Eric. The first time I saw him, I wanted his genes. I'd never felt that about a man before. I knew I'd have his baby. "I want to have a child with you," he whispered, back in bed at my place. "I do, too," I answered.

We came together fervently that night, gripping each other, saying, "I love you," at the exact same time. I was certain I'd conceived that night, especially because I wasn't using birth control—and sure enough, a couple of weeks later, a home pregnancy test confirmed it. My hand was shaking as I picked up the phone and called Amanda, telling her she had to come over. I lived just a few blocks from her place at the time. We met on the corner, and she hugged me tight. I was unable to contain myself.

"I had a feeling!" she said with a big smile. "You were glowing as you came down the street. Are you going to have it?" A look of concern spread across her face.

"Yes!" I put my hand on my stomach, totally sure and suddenly protective.

Of course, I was having this baby. *Why was she even asking?* I thought, feeling defensive. Yes, Amanda was my best friend, and she knew how dramatic and unpredictable life was with Eric. She was the one I called every time we broke up and got back together, which had already happened a few times in the year we'd been together. That wasn't much of a track record.

"Are you getting married?" Amanda asked. She was always realistic, which I usually appreciated. But now, I wanted to float away in a cloud of happiness and not face her concerns.

She wanted me to slow down and think about what I was doing. Eric was a hard-drinking construction worker from the Bronx, and I was a book-loving suburban girl from Northern California. Moreover, Eric was alcoholic and bipolar, which had already caused me pain. We'd been through a lot. But forever the idealist, I believed we could make it together, that our black-and-white family could withstand anything—from whispered bedtime quarrels to racist comments hurled at us as an interracial couple.

I was incredibly naive. And in love.

We felt that having a baby together would seal our love. Neither Eric nor I wanted to get married. We'd both been married and divorced before. (I was only twenty-two when I married my Spanish boyfriend so we could live in New York City together. I got divorced just one year later.)

I wanted this child. It was that simple. I was sure the human being inside me was the best thing that had ever happened to me. Nothing anyone said was going to change my mind.

The night of the rooftop party, I conceived not *just* Mae, but my whole idea of a family. And I was not about to let go of it. Reality be damned. I saw the three of us—mama, papa, and baby—sleeping together in one big bed, snuggled up all night long. On Sundays, Eric would bring me coffee and a mushroom and onion omelet on a tray. After that, the good daddy would take his big girl outside to play hopscotch and toss softballs in the back yard. We'd go camping together at the hot springs, listening to the Beatles as we drove along winding roads. At night, he and I would make a seamless transition and become lovers again, sneaking sex in the dark. I envisioned the triangle we'd be, the three of us holding each other up.

What was I thinking?

Now, almost two years after telling Amanda I was pregnant, I pull on a black silk skirt with a slit cut high up my thigh, a skimpy black tank top, and knee-high black boots with thick heels. This is my one sexy outfit, cobbled together from my sparse, all-black, pre-baby wardrobe. Not only have I not gone out on a date in that time, I haven't been clothes shopping either, except for Mae.

When I come out of the bathroom, I find Amanda and Mae lying in our bed. Mae bounces up when she sees me: "Milk!"

"Here you go, sweetie," I say, stretching out on the quilt and undoing my bra.

I lift my shirt up and Mae flies across the bed, latching on. I love nursing her. I imagine nursing her forever.

"You look stunning!" Amanda says.

"I do?" Here I am, my top hiked up to my neck and my boobs popping out. I don't feel stunning.

"But you look nervous," she says.

"Actually, I feel nauseous. I don't know if I can do this."

I've never left Mae at night like this. Sure, I'm only going three blocks away to a neighborhood bar. But this is before the days of online dating and Match.com. I have no experience meeting strangers like this, even ones who come with a trusted-neighbor guarantee. I've never even seen a picture of him. How will I recognize him?

"I better go," I say, as I glance at the clock.

I kiss Mae six times across her face and head.

"No," she says, clinging to my breasts.

"One more sip, sweetie," I say, feeling edgy and nervous. I don't want to go after all. It feels wrong to pull away and leave my baby. Maybe I should just call him and cancel.

"You're going to be late," Amanda says.

"I don't care."

But that's rude, I think. And it has been forever since I had a drink with a man. I take a deep breath and kiss Mae three more times on the top of her head.

"I love you," I say, and gently roll away from her.

It's hard to leave her, but still, I want to dash away, get drunk, and knock back a man.

I take the stairs down to the lobby. I always take the elevator with Mae, so it's invigorating to pound down the stairs in my high-heeled boots. Suddenly, I feel sexy and in charge, my MOM button temporarily set on PAUSE.

But when I step into the lobby, Raul, the building manager, is there.

"Rachel!" he says.

"Oh, hi—"

"You're all dressed up."

He looks me up and down, and I blush. Raul has never seen me dressed like this—usually I'm in sweats. Ever since that day he escorted me into the apartment to sign the lease, we seem to bump into each other a lot.

Raul has made it clear that he's divorced and devoted to his ten-year-old son who he has shared custody of. There's no chemistry between us, but I like his company. (Years later, I'll count him as one of the first men to become part of my close, platonic male tribe. He even made us a traditional El Salvadoran dinner one night recently; in between stirring a pot of rice and beans on the stove, he chased Mae around the apartment, calling her "my little guacamole.")

"Where's Mae?" he asks.

"Upstairs," I answer, feeling mortified. *What kind of mother are you, leaving your little girl so you can go on a blind date?*

What if he asks me where I'm going? Or who I'm planning to meet? Maybe I should just turn around and call this whole thing off.

"I was just on my way to my car," Raul says. "Do you need a ride?"

"Oh, no," I say. How awkward would that be: my cute building manager driving me to meet my blind date?

"Okay then, have a good time."

"Thanks so much."

I wave goodbye and push the door open. But part of me wants to stay inside where it's comfortable and familiar and chat with Raul. And where my baby is only an elevator ride away.

Outside, I breathe in the cold air. I'm strutting down the street in my boots and tight skirt, but I don't feel very hot. I stop and look down. Did I remember to shave both of my legs? Damn! I only shaved the right one.

What am I doing? I don't know how to date. Now I'm ten minutes late and too hurried to feel languid and sexy.

I rush into the bar and look around. A man with wire-rimmed glasses stands up and smiles at me. I shake his hand. He looks much older than I'd imagined, with a receding hairline and lines under his eyes. My friends had promised he was handsome, but I don't really see it. *Darn.*

"It's so good to meet you," Mark says, touching my arm.

He leaves his hand on my elbow for a long moment. I stop breathing. Then he immediately takes charge, ordering two margaritas and carrying them to a table in the corner. I follow behind him, checking out his tight little butt. *Alright, he's not so bad. I can do this.*

"So, you have a daughter?" Mark asks.

"Yeah," I say, "she's about to turn one."

"She must be adorable."

Boy, he's really saying all the right things.

"She is," I say. "I'm late because I was nursing her before bed—"

"You were nursing her?"

Wait, is that a sparkle I see in his eyes? I nod my head and take a big gulp of my drink.

"A woman who's lactating!" he says way too loudly. "What a turn-on!"

I wait for the punch line, but he's not joking.

I'm flattered and freaked out at the same time. Here's a man who's unperturbed by a woman who nurses her child longer than six months (the norm in the United States). This earns him extra points, though he may not have even picked up on it. But what does he mean when he says that he's turned on? Does he have some weird fetish for lactating women?

He gets up to order another margarita. I'm still sipping my first one. All of a sudden, my breasts are flooding with milk. This happens whenever I think about nursing Mae. The milk lets down, something I have no control over. I look down, and there's a damp spot on my chest. I'm leaking. This is just a tad embarrassing.

But I'm hungry for a bit of intimate conversation with a man. I don't care if he's thin and tired-looking. I just want a night of some no-strings fun.

"Do you smoke pot?" Mark asks when he comes back.

"No!" I exclaim loud enough so that people look over. Doesn't he know the effects of marijuana on a growing baby? And more important, isn't this an odd question for the beginning of a first date?

He leans across the table, only inches away from me. "You're really cute," he says.

I giggle. His attention feels good—even if he's a little odd. Give me a few years, and I won't be so desperate for attention. But right now, I'm enjoying the moment. We gossip about my neighbors and his latest legal aid case. I give him the details of Mae's all-natural, easy birth. All the while, I'm thinking, *Will I sleep with him?* He doesn't seem trustworthy. But who cares about trust when it's just a one-night stand?

My breasts are swelling now. The wet circle on my blouse has grown bigger. I cross my arms to cover it up. I've got to get home. When I glance down at my watch, it's almost midnight.

I told Amanda I'd be home by now. All I can think about is the fact I have to get back to Mae.

I've had just one drink—but he's had two, and he's driving home.

"Look, you've had a lot to drink," I say, "and we didn't eat anything—"

"I'm fine," he says.

"No, I don't feel right about it."

"Really, I'll be fine," he says.

But I say: "Why don't you walk me home and come upstairs for an hour to let the alcohol wear off?"

He beams. "Sure, if you say so!"

As we walk back to my place, he wraps his arm around me, gently pulling me to his side. I'm a little off balance in my boots—it's the alcohol and the fact that I haven't worn heels for over a year—but he holds me up.

It feels good to be steadied by a man, even if it's a guy I'm not excited about. Sure, I could do better. But at this moment, he's nice, and it feels so good to lean against him.

My life as a single mom feels like sitting on one end of a teeter-totter, holding my baby tightly. We're weighed down and heavy, smack against the ground. But there's no one on the other side. I wish I had a man there, keeping us balanced.

When I unlock the door to my apartment, Amanda is stretched out on a pillow in the living room with a book. She sits up quickly, startled by the fact that I'm *not* alone.

"Amanda, this is Mark," I say, as if there's nothing unusual about bringing a strange man home, a man I met just two hours ago at a bar.

Mark takes a big step toward Amanda and offers his hand.

"Uh, hi," she says, getting to her feet, and looking at me aghast.

"How did it go with my girl?" I ask.

"She cried a little, but I rocked her and she fell asleep."

"She cried?" The guilt sets in swiftly. *She cried? This is all wrong. I stayed out too long. I should never have gone.*

"Don't worry, it was just a little whimper," Amanda says.

I exhale.

"It looks like you two had fun," she says directly to me, without taking her eyes off mine.

I know exactly what she's thinking: *What the hell are you doing, Rachel? You just met this guy, and you're bringing him home? Your daughter is sleeping in the next room!*

"He's just come in for a bite to eat," I say, patting her arm.

But she looks skeptical: *A bite of what to eat?*

Amanda has always told me that I move way too fast with men. "You're always in such a hurry to sleep together," she has said over the years.

It's not like I have a master plan to sleep with a man on the first or second date. But holding off doesn't come as easy for me as it does for her. Amanda is the kind of woman who can take sex or leave it; I think we are wired differently.

When the opportunity to be touched and held is right in front of me, I jump on it. I love the charge I get when I'm with a man. It's more than that, though. Whenever I feel lonely, it's hard to hold myself. I don't know how to contain my intense solitude. When a man holds me, it's an instant fix. I melt at his touch.

Fine then, let him hold you, Amanda has told me. *But you don't have to take your clothes off right away.* She has a point: Why can't I wait? She has dated men for months before sleeping with them. I want that instant intimacy, even if it's potentially damaging to a relationship down the line.

The three of us stand silently in my little living room, immobile; finally, Amanda moves toward the door. As she pulls on her coat, I step away from Mark to give her a hug. I know exactly what she wants: She's dying to pull me into the hallway to whisper-shout her warning. She cares about me. She wants me to be cautious.

As Amanda reaches for the doorknob, I put my hand on her shoulder. As I suspected, she pulls me close and whispers, "Please be safe."

I squeeze her extra tight, as if to say, *I will.*

As soon as she leaves, Mark reaches out and wraps his arms around me. "You have beautiful eyes," he says.

"Thank—" I say, but he stops me with his lips. Our mouths meet softly, and I open mine to his. I love a man who knows how to kiss, and Mark does. His lips touch mine, smoothly, and we enfold each other. Still, my torso stiffens. *Isn't he moving a little fast? Shouldn't we sit down and chat for a bit?*

I want to press the PAUSE button and leave him for a moment to check on my baby girl. I haven't even peeked at her. I want to see her sleeping. But Mark is gripping my hips. I pull my mouth away from his.

"Just a second," I say, backing away.

"Not yet," Mark says.

His lips slowly move down my neck, as he gently runs his tongue across the nape. His hands hold my back tenderly, and I feel his fingers move down to my ass.

Suddenly, I hear a little cry coming from the bedroom.

"Just a second," I say to Mark, really pulling away from him this time.

Quietly, I push open the bedroom door and peer in at Mae. She's dreaming, crying out softly in her sleep. Amanda made a safe barrier of pillows around her on my bed, so Mae won't fall to the floor. I say a silent prayer: *Please sleep, honey pie.*

I have no idea how simple things are right now. Mae is just a baby, not walking yet, and hardly able to climb down from the bed by herself. She's so little that she can't do something as simple as open a door—she can barely reach the knob. It's easy to bring a man home secretly like this. I have no clue how tricky things will become a few years from now when I want to do this.

"*Mmmmm,* you taste so good," Mark says when we get back to kissing. He reaches out and unbuttons my blouse. He runs his mouth across the edge of my bra. I know that I should reach back and unfasten it, but things are progressing more rapidly than I'd imagined.

I reach out and stroke his hair.

"You are so hot," Mark says, and I feel it.

I really do, but my head is racing. It's been a long time since a man touched my breasts. It feels so good, but I also feel uneasy. *What if my baby wakes up? What if he asks to stay until the morning? Maybe this was all a terrible idea. Should I ask him to leave?*

He licks his finger and slowly circles my large brown nipple.

"I'm sorry I don't have anywhere for us to lie down," I whisper.

"Right here is just fine," he says, guiding me to the rug on the living room floor. He hungrily kisses my breast, and I realize that I'm leaking.

I'm embarrassed. "I'm sorry, but—"

He bends over me and eagerly sucks on my nipple. I freeze. *Hold on there, buddy, this is my daughter's milk!* My back stiffens, and I push him back. *You're wasting this precious gold! How dare you!*

"I've never tasted anything so sweet in my life," he says, looking into my eyes. I can't tell if he's horny or sincere, or both. But the truth is, this does feel good. My breasts are begging to be touched softly like this. He doesn't nibble on me like my baby does. He's a world apart from my baby, who sucks hard, her mouth inflexible.

On second thought, he is coming at me with the same voraciousness as my baby. *Isn't this immoral? A man is drinking my little baby's milk!* My mind races, trying to grasp what's happening. *This milk is coming from my body, isn't it? So, it must be mine, right?*

"Do you like it?" I ask.

"I love it." He softly licks my nipple again.

"You do?" Maybe he does have some strange nursing fetish. Maybe his mother never breastfed him.

"You are so sweet, do you know that?" He's smiling at me.

I arch my back slightly, offering myself to him. He softly sucks my other breast. It's pure bliss. How can I deny him? *Go for it, drink to your heart's delight,* I think.

And he does.

On Friday night, before my second date with Mark, I'm tense and edgy. I've been nursing Mae for over an hour and she won't go to sleep.

"Please," I say.

She pops off my nipple and grins at me as if we have all the time in the world. But we don't. Mark will be here any minute, and I'm still not ready. I need to shower, exfoliate, and ready myself for a hot night. On our date last weekend, I must have channeled Amanda: I passed up the chance for some sex, even though it had been so long. We did everything but—and it was blissful. We were skin to skin, wet, hot, and ready to roll. Mae was sleeping peacefully in her room—all systems go.

Then I said, "Not yet." Where did *that* voice come from? I can't recall the number of times I've jumped on a wild night like this one, at least pre-Mae. Although I'm proud of myself for not sleeping with Mark on our first date, part of me still regrets it. I haven't slept with anyone since Eric. It's been almost a year, unless you count that last hurrah with Eric before he split town.

Luckily, Mark called a few nights ago, asking if we might get together again and pick up where we left off. After we got off the phone, I thought, *You better believe that I'm going all the way next time.*

But what stopped me last week? Pre-baby, I would definitely have slept with Mark on the first date. Pre-baby, I brought men like him home for a quick, yet always safe and responsible let's-get-it-on. I'd had sexy adventures around the globe—Mexico, the Czech Republic, Spain, New York. Pre-baby, I was the kind of woman who made rash—and often not smart—decisions about men. *I want to sleep with you, here's a condom, thank you very much.*

Was my heart ever broken? Yes.

Did I want to hold on to certain men forever? Yes.

But did I ever tell a man, "Not yet"?

Uh, never.

Though I've been adventurous, I've never been a one-night-stand kind of woman. I like the company, just the simple company of a man. I like being touched and craved. I like hearing a man say, "Hi, sweetie." I like knowing he's there when I'm sad or vulnerable. I like how his stubble feels against my neck; I like dinner conversations and road trips. I like sinking into his body at night. I like opening my eyes in the morning and seeing him there.

When I connect with a man physically, I don't want to let him go.

But for now, Mae doesn't want to loosen her hold on me, and Mark will be here soon. My nipples are sore; my shoulders tense. Do I really want an all-night sex marathon? Suddenly a nap seems much more appealing. Or maybe I want more than just sex. Hell, I don't know even what I want.

One thing I know for a fact: Motherhood has changed me. It's definitely not just about me and whatever man strikes my fancy. It's just as much about Mae. What I ultimately want is a meaningful connection with a man, a heartfelt bond that lingers in the morning. But I'm not there yet. The post-Eric hole in my heart is still wide open, and I'm not letting another man in. Not yet.

"Mama?" Mae says, looking into my eyes.

"What honey?" Lost in my thoughts, I'm surprised to hear her voice.

"Mama?" she says again, smiling.

She has nothing to say. She simply wants to stay awake.

I say, *Shhhhh.*

Shhhhh, she mimics me, pursing her lips together.

How in the world can you force a nursing toddler to sleep? The answer: You can't. What do other nursing single moms do on their way out the door? Good question, and I don't think I'm going to figure it out tonight.

I wrap my arm around her and gently rock her. The movement is so soothing that my own eyelids get heavy. I haven't had a full night's sleep in over a year. Mae wakes up every few hours to nurse, and I feel depleted. What I really need to do tonight is curl up next to my little girl and get some rest. My long brown hair is uncombed, and I'm wearing no makeup. I have on one of Eric's old T-shirts. Mae pokes her tiny finger through a hole in it.

I glance at the clock. It's 9:30. *There's a man on his way here to see me!* I want to sing. *A man! A man!* I need to rouse myself and get psyched for this—and hope Mae falls asleep soon.

I'm *not* supposed to have sex with a man while my baby is sleeping in the next room. This will be a totally new experience for me, and one I'm not comfortable with. As if there isn't already enough to worry about the first time I'm with a new man.

Why didn't I just get a baby sitter and go over to Mark's place? Wouldn't that have simplified things? But then I would have worried about Mae all night—definitely not a libido enhancer. And since Mae still wakes up at night to nurse, it's not exactly practical. Most important, I can still hear her in the next room if she cries, which will pull me away from anything, including the best sex.

"Mama?" she says again.

"Sleep," I say.

I play her game and close my eyes, too, pretending to be asleep. I count to ten. Then I slowly open one eye and look at her: She's still wide awake and twirling her little hands in the air.

Meanwhile, I'm hoping there's a delay on the A train. My eyes are glued to the clock: 9:35, 9:39, 9:43. A siren blares in the distance. The neighbor's dog barks. When I peer down at Mae, her eyes are closed. *Sleep, oh, gracious sleep.* I get up quietly, and she puckers her lips in the air but doesn't wake up.

Then, as if on cue, I hear a knock on the door. Careful not to disturb Mae, I find a pair of Levi's on the floor and pull them on.

Knock, knock, knock.

I comb my hair with my fingers. I'll have to forgo makeup. I'm grateful for the darkness of night.

When I open the door, Mark is clutching a big comforter.

"Don't worry," he says. "I'm not moving in."

"Excuse me?" I don't get the joke.

"I just brought it so we'll be comfortable on the floor," he says. "I remembered that you don't have a sofa."

"Oh, that's so sweet of you."

I'm so nervous that it takes a moment for his little joke to register. I get it now: He's brought extra padding to make sure we're cozy on my hardwood floor. Suddenly he looks a little like a kid showing up for naptime at his preschool. I try not to giggle.

He steps into my living room and kisses the top of my head. *What a sweetheart.* I know I'm *not* supposed to think mushy thoughts like this about this guy. I'm *not* supposed to get attached to him.

"I missed you," he says as he takes his glasses off and perches them on top of my TV.

"You did?"

My heart is pounding as I look at him, at the gentle way that he spreads the blanket on the floor, smoothing the corners just right. He stands up, and we kiss, our mouths open, hungry. Quickly, he pulls off my T-shirt. When he tugs at my panties, I step out of them. I hold my breath as I reach out and undo his belt buckle. His khaki pants fall around his ankles. He raises his arms in the air, and I tug his shirt off. I'm working mechanically, as if I'm a mother undressing her kid before bed. I've done this hundreds of times. I need to switch gears here.

But it's been so long since I took a *man's* clothes off. Shouldn't I be undoing his buttons with my teeth? Shouldn't I be sucking on his fingers, teasing him? I don't remember how to do this seductively.

I lie down on the floor and stretch out on his comforter. It's scratchy on my back, certainly not the 100 percent organic cotton I insist my baby girl sleep on. He joins me, leaning over to kiss my neck, my breasts, my belly button. He nibbles on my inner thighs, and I open up my legs and moan loudly.

A few seconds later, we hear, *Waaaaaaa!*

Mae. Could I have woken her up?

Bad mama.

I hold my head up and listen closely. I hear nothing.

Get up. Check on her.

I should. I really should. But I'm hot and wet and ready for him. And it's been so long. His tongue glides across my clit, then lightly flickers. I want to cry out, but don't dare. He guides his cock over my thighs, tempting me. I reach down and grip him gently, stroking.

"Ah, that feels good—"

"Do you have a condom?" I ask.

I should have a box on hand. What was I thinking, inviting a man over and *not* buying any condoms?

"Of course," he says, feeling in the dark for his jeans. He hands it to me.

You've got to be kidding. I don't remember how to put one of these things on. I haven't used one for at least a year. Mark holds me close, gripping my hips with both hands. He's ready and waiting. I unroll the condom and stretch it out. Is this how it works? My fingers are shaking.

I feel him getting soft in my hand. *Oh please, don't do that.*

I strain to see as I put the condom on. I've got to remember how this works.

"C'mon, Rachel," he says, tugging on my arm.

I straddle him. He slides inside me.

"I'm all yours," I whisper.

If I weren't so caught up in my sleep-deprived fantasy, I would notice that he does not want to be mine. I would open my eyes and know that this is simply sex to him, nothing more. But I see none of this right now.

A few minutes of moving on top of him is all it takes. I go over the edge and fall on his chest. When I exhale, there's a triangle in my mind, the three of us—mama, papa, and baby—together in one big bed. I want it all: a man who will join us to make a congruent triangle. The three of us will hold each other up. Yes, the triangle is what I want. This is my postorgasmic fantasy.

Mark silently slips out the door at 3 AM.

He doesn't say, "I'll call you."

He doesn't say, "I'll see you soon."

He says nothing. But what did I expect? C'mon, when have I ever been able to take sex lightly? After all, a night of no-strings sex had been my idea. If only my heart would listen to my mind.

The next morning, Mae wakes me at sunrise. After three hours of sleep, I'm groggy. Still caught up in last night, I close my eyes as Mae nurses and replay having sex with Mark.

I can always count on Mae to ground me. When I open my eyes, I look at the calendar on the wall; there's a big circle around April 4. My baby is turning a year old next week. That's big. I want to have a little party here at our sofa-less place, but I dread doing it alone.

How am I supposed to throw my daughter her very first birthday party all by myself? It's supposed to be a family affair: You and your partner sit down and make a list. *You pick up the vanilla cake at the bakery and make sure they spell her name right; I'll get the paper plates and streamers on my way home.*

It doesn't feel right to sit at the kitchen table alone, the solitary organizer deciding whom to invite and which snacks to serve. Sometimes I think that maybe, just maybe, there will be a knock at the door, and Eric will walk back into our lives.

The phone rings. I jump out of bed. My father is calling from Boynton Beach, Florida, where he's moved temporarily from San Francisco to be closer to his mother and sister. My ninety-two-year-old grandmother has been saying for over a year, "I don't want to live anymore! Take me away!" His sister, my Aunt Myrna, is having chemo again, as she continues to battle cancer. My father wants to be there for the women in his family, including me and Mae.

"Someone has a birthday coming up!" my dad says. Although he has met his granddaughter only a couple of times, he's a doting long-distance grandpa.

"Can you believe it, Dad?"

"Why don't you come down here for the weekend?" he asks.

"To Florida?"

"Why not?"

"I don't think so, Dad . . ."

The last thing I want is to be surrounded by my dad's side of my family for Mae's first birthday. They tend to be dramatic and loud. I can see them noisily vying for each other's attention, ignoring Mae.

Think of a friendly Woody Allen with a Boston accent. That's my dad. We've always had an intense relationship. Even so, he's the one man I can always count on. No matter what kind of life emergencies I get myself into, my dad always comes to the rescue. This is true right now, when I'm feeling disappointed by Mark's rude departure last night. And it was certainly true when Eric walked out the door. When I called my dad to tell him, he immediately wanted to fly out to be with Mae and me. "As a parent, I wish I could just wave the magic wand," he said.

The week before Thanksgiving 2000, Eric told me he wouldn't be coming with us to my cousin's house in Massachusetts, where we planned to spend the holiday. Instead, he wanted to stay in New York to be with his sisters on Thanksgiving, something he hadn't done for more than a decade. At that point, our two-year relationship had hit a particularly rough patch, and we were arguing a lot. I thought a brief time apart would do us good.

The day before Thanksgiving, Eric took us to Penn Station as planned. He walked us to the train, gave the baby and me a quick peck on the cheek, and stepped away just as the doors were closing.

That was the last time we saw him.

The morning after Thanksgiving, I called home to see how his Thanksgiving had been and to remind him to meet our train the next day. There was no answer. As I left a message, giving him our arrival time, I had a bad feeling. Why wasn't he home at 7 AM?

When we got off the train, he wasn't there.

I found a pay phone and called Eric's younger sister in Harlem. She told me he hadn't shown up for Thanksgiving. My head started throbbing. Something was really wrong.

"Don't worry," she said. "I'll call Joseph and tell him to come and get you."

Joseph was Eric's older brother, the dependable one in their family. Though I'd met him only a handful of times, he had always been interested in how Eric, Mae, and I were doing. And I suspect he knew that things were not going well.

Joseph arrived within a half hour, embracing Mae with one hand and patting me on the shoulder with the other. He scooped up Mae's car seat and our suitcase and said, "C'mon girls, let's go."

When we arrived at our apartment, I was certain Eric would be there. With Mae on my hip, I rushed from room to room, looking for a clue, a note, anything that said why he wasn't there. I discovered that he'd taken all his clothes from the closet. But he left the photos of Mae and him, the one of her fast asleep on his chest in bed and the one of them cuddling on a blanket at our neighborhood park. He'd left his carpentry tools, too.

This meant he was coming back, right?

It would take a year for it to finally sink in: Eric wasn't coming home.

Two weeks after Eric disappeared, I woke up in the middle of the night, itching all over. I propped pillows alongside Mae in our big bed and went to the bathroom to look in the mirror: Red hives covered my arms, belly, and thighs. My body was telling me, *You're in shock, honey.*

The next time Joseph called to see how we were doing, I stopped pretending that everything was okay.

"Actually, I'm having a hard time," I said, trying my best to hold back tears. "I can't stay here. I'm going to start looking for a new place."

There was silence on the other end, and then Joseph said, "Let me take you girls out for Chinese food."

At the restaurant, we squeezed into a table between two other families, both with children under three. After taking our order, the waitress said to Joseph, "Your daughter is beautiful!"

"Thank you," he bowed his head.

"Sure, go ahead and take full credit," I teased him after the waitress left. But really, I didn't mind at all: I was enjoying this moment of feeling like we were a real family out for dinner together. Joseph and Mae looked more alike than she and Eric did: their cinnamon skin, large foreheads, full lips, defined noses.

When he suggested during dinner that he thought Mae and I should stay with him, I was taken aback, but also relieved. "Stay with *you*?" I'd only been in his apartment a couple of times for family get-togethers. It was a big one-bedroom in Harlem, dimly lit and dusty, with African statues and free weights everywhere.

"Until you get your feet on the ground," Joseph said. "I have a huge place. Why don't you just stay with me until you find a new apartment?"

"Are you sure?" I was touched.

I was paying a lot for the two-bedroom where we lived, a winding place where it was getting hard to keep my eyes on Mae.

Joseph wrapped his big hands around Mae and pulled her gently onto his lap. "Of course I'm sure," he said in a sugary voice, looking into her eyes.

Uncle Joseph is one of the first guests to arrive at Mae's first birthday party, one week after my hot date with Mark. Of course, my friend Amanda is there, and our neighbors Susan and Jim, and Mae's aunts on Eric's side.

The next morning, we're off to Florida.

Aunt Myrna, who has never met Mae, offers to throw a little party in her back yard. And my dad has already gone to Toys "R" Us to buy gifts. When they pick us up at the airport, my aunt sings "The Wheels on the Bus" to Mae the whole way home. Mae can't take her eyes off my aunt, whom I haven't seen for years. I never knew that she was so good with little kids.

The day of the party, my grandma arrives. She had yelled and screamed at me on the phone when she found out I was pregnant and not married to the father, who happened to be African American. "Give me that baby!" she now says with a smile.

I hand Mae over, but stick right by my grandma's side.

"Oh, you sweet little baby," my grandma coos. I can't believe how much she's warmed to her. But then again, my grandma has nothing against Mae, really. I was the one who disappointed her.

"Oh, you beautiful girl," my grandma says as she bounces Mae on her knees.

Mae giggles.

"She's too skinny," my grandma says. "Get me some turkey—"

"Grandma, she doesn't eat turkey yet."

"Get me some turkey! She *must* eat."

This is the craziness I have to deal with when I visit my family.

My first night here, I long for Mark. We had sex only once, and already I'm attached, just like a true woman. I get up to call him. As I dial his number, I vow to sound casual and nonchalant. His voice mail picks up.

"Hi, it's Rachel. How are you?" I say, leaving a message.

I try hard to lift my voice happily: "We're having a great time here in sunny Florida!"

I sound like an idiot.

I've opened myself up to him, and I need him right now. I need his voice. I need his reassurance. I need to know that I'll see him when I get back. But I realize that this is an unfair expectation. One night of sex and suddenly he's supposed to save me? I need to get real. The next day, I check my cell phone every hour. There's no word from Mark.

I leave him another message: "Just calling again to check in . . ."

I imagine us having phone sex at night, rubbing myself under the covers as my father snores down the hall. I'm a fool.

The next afternoon, when I get back from the swimming pool, my phone is flashing. There's a message.

"Uh, hi. It's Mark. Glad you're having fun."

His voice is emotionless and flat. *That's it?*

I put Mae down for her nap. Then I shut myself in the bathroom and dial his number.

He answers on the fourth ring.

"How are you doing?" I ask.

"Great."

"Really? What are you up to?"

"Just cleaning my place," he says. "I'm tired."

"Are you having fun without me?" I ask.

"I guess," he says.

"What did you do last night?"

"I went out for dinner with my brother last night, and we drank a lot."

"Your brother was in town?" I recall that his brother lives upstate.

"Yeah."

"That must have been nice," I say. "What's his name?"

"Greg."

Why don't I notice that most of his responses are just one word? Can I not hear the total lack of interest in his voice? Am I that out of tune?

After precisely three minutes, we say goodbye and hang up. I want to lie down and take a long nap. I want to walk along the beach alone.

My dad takes everyone out for dinner. I want to tell him about Mark. I want to tell him that I'm lonely. My dad doesn't even know that I went on my first single-motherhood date. But dinner is no place for this. My aunt is pale from the chemo. My grandma snaps at the waiter. Mae drops her spoon to the floor over and over.

That night, Mark calls again.

"Rachel?"

"Yeah?"

"Look," he says. "I wasn't really honest with you—"

"What do you mean?"

"I didn't have dinner with my brother last night," he says.

"You didn't?" I say.

"I didn't have dinner at all. I slept with a woman I used to have something with last year."

Something with?

"Thanks for telling me," I say.

"Well, I'm glad we got that out of the way," he says.

I want to say, "See you, buddy."

I want to say, "You're an asshole."

Instead, I say, simply, "I have to go."

A few days later, we're back in New York City, riding the subway. When I open my backpack to pull out a book to read to Mae, I find a surprise. It's a little gift I'd picked up for her birthday and had forgotten to give to her. I pull it out: an African American baby doll with a plastic head and cloth body.

Mae takes her from me and peers into her little brown eyes. Then she bends her head forward and starts kissing the plastic face. Her lips pucker up: *Smack! Smack!*

The woman next to me giggles. Then two men in suits sitting across from us crack up.

Mae keeps kissing and kissing. She seems to know exactly what love is.

And what do I know about love? Love hurts. Love has bruised me like a peach left in a plastic grocery bag that bumped against my leg all day. No one wants to touch it now. It's going in the garbage.

But there's always the prospect of a new peach, smooth and fresh, waiting for you to take a big, expectant bite out of it—just like life.

Chapter Three: Who's Your Daddy?

"I want to let you know about a friend of mine, a real cool guy from Chapel Hill who just moved to the Big Apple," says the email from Lawrence, my ex-boyfriend, whom I lived with after I dropped out of college when I was eighteen.

Lawrence recently moved to France with his girlfriend, and we've stayed in touch over the years. "My friend is a local math teacher," Lawrence writes. "His name is Victor."

I read his name over and over. *Victor.* I like the sound of that. *Victor, as in Victory.* He's a fighter, a winner, a defeater, a champion. He'll be upbeat and optimistic.

Spring and summer have passed. It's a month after September 11, 2001, when I send Victor a short email, explaining that I got his name from our mutual friend. I ask how he likes New York.

The next day, there's a reply. He starts off with a little song: *Bee bop, da da da. . . .*

How cute is that? I think.

Victor writes that he arrived in New York from North Carolina just a couple of weeks before September 11. He's a junior high math teacher in a tough neighborhood in East New York. He hasn't unpacked his bags yet.

I ask if he wants to meet my daughter and me in the park one Friday afternoon. I realize this must sound strange, offering to meet some cute guy for a date, and then dragging my baby along for the ride. But in the wake of 9/11, I don't want to leave Mae alone, even with a baby sitter.

"Sure, kid," he says in his email. Kid? When's the last time someone called me a kid? I like how warm I feel when he says that. But I wonder how old he is. Anyone who calls me "kid" must be in his forties, for sure.

Victor writes that he'll hop on the train after his last class ends at three o'clock.

On Friday afternoon, I pull on a pair of faded blue jeans and a ruffled Guatemalan top. I smear on some liquid makeup and a coat of lipstick. I'm jittery, but in a good way. Eighteen-month-old Mae and I leave the apartment in sandals, without jackets. It's an Indian summer day, and the humidity has spread thick into the fall.

As Mae toddles along the sidewalk to the park, I look up and see Otis's UPS truck. I still get all nervous and shaky whenever I see him and his lovely forearms. I'm trying to keep cool right now. There's no future for us, but I still think he's cute.

Get a grip, I think.

"Otis truck!" Mae says. Whenever she sees his truck, she gets excited.

Like mother, like daughter.

Mae pokes her little head into the driver's side. "Hi?" she says.

It's empty; he must be delivering a package.

"Otis isn't there, honey," I say.

"Wake it up?" she asks.

Oh, my cutie-pie. She wants to wake the truck up and watch it go.

"C'mon, Mae, let's go to the park." I steer her toward the playground. At this age, she's still easily distracted.

I'm *totally* distracted. I walk along and wonder, *What will Victor look like? What will his voice sound like? Will he have dark or light eyes?* We haven't even talked on the phone.

"*Wee!*" Mae screams, pointing to the swings. I plop her into the baby swing and check my watch. We did say 4:30, right?

I sing the ABCs. Then I sing them again. Ten minutes pass, then fifteen. Where is he? The ice cream truck on the corner plays the same tune over and over. I make up a little song in my head, *Victor, oh, Victor, please come and score a victory.*

I check my watch again. Maybe I got the time mixed up? Maybe I got the days all mixed up? Is he going to stand me up? He doesn't have a cell phone. My armpits are sweaty. Is he really going to stand me up? I don't even *know* this guy, and I'm already afraid he's going to leave me. Not good. Not good at all. A couple of big kids with melting Popsicles saunter over to the swings. The ever-observant Mae is quick to notice them.

"Pop!" she says, pointing to their Popsicles.

I scoop her into my arms, feeling defeated. She's so easy. A cold Popsicle is all she needs to make her happy. I carry Mae and her lemon Popsicle to a park bench that faces the A train exit. She settles onto my lap. I check my watch again.

Half an hour has passed. *Face it, girl, you've been stood up.* All of a sudden, a young man rushes up the stairs, looking panicked. He's boyish, with adorable round cheeks, café skin, and full lips. He waves to me. I wave back. As he walks through the playground gates, all hope is restored. It's as if the sky above me has opened and sprinkled magic dust upon my head.

"I'm so sorry," Victor says. "Rush hour! It took an hour and a half to get here from Brooklyn."

I reach out my hand, sticky with Popsicle juice. "Thanks so much for making the trip." Does my sticky hand gross him out? "I'm sorry about the stickiness," I say.

"That's okay," he says. "It's really nice to meet you."

I smile. When he sits down next to me on the bench, our knees touch. We slide into small talk about our mutual friend and the horrors of September 11.

"And your husband?" Victor asks.

"My husband?"

"Is he here?" Victor says.

"Didn't Lawrence tell you that I'm single?"

Oops.

"No, he didn't," Victor says, smiling. "You're divorced?"

"Not exactly," I say in a whisper, not wanting Mae to hear. "Her father stepped off."

"Stepped off?"

I still don't know how to explain this part to strangers. Do I start with the fact that Eric is manic-depressive? Or, that he's an alcoholic? Do I simply tell the story, about how we came home one day and he was just gone? Maybe "stepped off" isn't the right term. It sounds like he died. I could say that he vanished. I could say that he's nowhere to be found.

"We came home one day and he was gone," I try again. "He had a lot of problems."

"I'm sorry," Victor says.

"Don't be."

A mother and her toddler join us on the bench.

"You have such a beautiful baby," the mother says to Victor.

"Oh no, she's not *my* baby," Victor says.

I try to hold back laughter.

"We're just friends," Victor says.

I look down at Mae, who's slurping her Popsicle. Their skin color is almost identical. They *could* be related.

A month earlier, on September 11, I am wading into the swimming pool with Mae at the YMCA on 63rd Street when the lifeguard bends down on one knee and says, "A plane has just hit one of the World Trade towers."

A mother turns to me in the water. We both shake our heads. *How awful. What a horrible accident . . .*

The lifeguard tells everyone to exit the pool. The YMCA has strict orders to close its doors and send everyone home. I'm confused: If this is just an accident, why do we have to leave? We're in the Upper West Side, after all, nowhere close to the towers. I lift Mae out and wrap her in a towel, then follow the other mothers into the locker room.

But Mae squirms in my arms. "Walk," she says.

At seventeen months, she is independent and strong willed. I grip her little body with tense fingers. I am not ready to let her go. "I wonder what's going on," I say to the mom next to me. She is tugging a turtleneck over her toddler's wet head.

"Do you think it was just an accident?" I ask, the mother in me superseded by the journalist in me. I am wondering what really happened as I hurry Mae out of her suit and into her clothes.

The place clears out within minutes. We all know that something indescribably horrible has happened. I just want to get to a TV or radio to see what it is.

When we get to the lobby, I check my cell phone. It is out of service. People line up at the pay phone—and that's when I get really scared. I think of calling Amanda, but I know she's at work. I decide to head home where I can learn more. I push Mae's stroller down the street only to find the subway has shut down. Ambulances roar past. Taxis honk; each one is occupied. People are running. When I look down, Mae has fallen asleep. With no way to get home right now, I feel lost.

I decide to walk around the corner to where Karen, a friend of a friend, lives. She has a two-year-old daughter who has played with Mae. I'm in luck; Karen is home.

"Rachel!" she says when the elevator opens. She holds her daughter, Lucy, in her arms. Desperate to find out what's going on, I push Mae's stroller through Karen's doorway. Her husband is watching TV in the living room. The image is shocking: planes ramming right into the Twin Towers. And now there are reports that both towers are down. This can't be real. Karen explains to me that this is *not* an accident—that this was carried out by terrorists.

I want my family right now. I usually speak to my dad every couple of weeks on the phone, but I haven't talked to my mom for months, since she went to Morocco on a Fulbright soon after Mae's birth. She is doing her own thing now, and I'm doing mine. Still, I wish I could call her right now, hear her voice and tell her we're okay.

By the evening, the subway is running again. I scoop Mae up, thank my friends, and head back out to the street. I just want to get home. I want to lie in bed and nurse Mae with my arm around her. We reach our apartment in the dark, and my answering machine is blinking. Raul, our sweet building manager, is the first to call.

"Rachel? Mae? Are you there? Please call me when you get home, okay?"

I am touched by everyone who has checked in to make sure we are safe: my dad; my sister from the Bay Area; Joseph, Eric's brother; Amanda, calling from work to say that we could take a cab down to her place in the East Village to spend the night.

I am grateful to hear their voices, but I still feel so alone. I bring Mae into bed and curl my body around her. I don't have the energy to head down to the Village. Mae and I fall asleep, but at 3 AM, I bolt awake. The phone is ringing.

I rush into the living room. "Hello?" I say.

"How are you, baby?"

It's Eric, on a crackly phone line.

"How did you get my number?"

"It doesn't matter."

"Where are you?" I ask.

"Europe," he says. He is vague, as always.

"Where in Europe?"

"It doesn't matter." I say nothing. But I'm wrenching inside. My hands shake. I lean against the wall and slide down it. I wish he were here right now to steady me.

"Are you girls all right?" Eric asks.

"Yes. Are you?"

"Yes, baby."

I hold my breath. *He left you. He walked out the door. Put down the phone right now. Say goodbye. Just hang up.*

"I'm worried about you."

"Yeah, I bet you're worried," I say sarcastically.

"C'mon, Rachel, please don't do that."

"If you're so worried, then what are you doing so far away?" I clench my jaw. I know I should hang up the phone.

"I'm coming back," he says.

"Sure you are," I say. My voice is cold and steely.

"I love you," he says.

The phone dies. Did he hang up on me? Did we lose our connection? There is no way I can call him back. I loosen my grip around the receiver and wait for the phone to ring. Tears fall down my cheeks. I wrap my arms around my knees.

He does not call back. But his voice weighs on me. Thoughts collide inside me all night. *Now he feels bad for leaving us, now that our country is under attack. He says he's coming back. Yeah, right.*

For weeks, I walk around in a daze, stopping to read the posters of the missing pasted on every street corner, with names and ages, heights and weights, and photos. I didn't know anyone who died that morning. I've heard about many friends of friends. Wives and husbands of World Trade Center workers trek around the city tacking photos up. I obsess about the wives, especially. They, too, have children, and these children have been abandoned.

Though I feel lucky that Eric is alive and that I know his approximate whereabouts, I feel abandoned too. I am grateful to the close friends I have here, but I feel lonely. Maybe it will take this tragedy for me to truly see that it's time to move on.

Victor and I are going on our real first date. He's invited me to an outdoor performance of Bertolt Brecht's *Mother Courage and Her Children* in Washington Square Park. Written in 1939, the play is an intense antiwar drama about a mother and her children during the Thirty Years' War in the seventeenth century. I'm touched by the fact that he's taking me to a play about a mother's extraordinary struggles. But to be honest, I wouldn't mind a trouble-free getaway with him right now, like sharing a bottle of wine on the pier while watching the sunset.

It's eight o'clock, and Victor will be here any minute. I'm nursing Mae on the air mattress in Amanda's East Village apartment. The play is a ten-minute walk from here. Amanda is an angel to baby-sit. My blouse is unbuttoned, and both breasts hang out. *Let's party,* they seem to say.

"Honey, Mommy's going out for a little while," I say to Mae.

"No!" She pops off my breast and looks into my eyes.

"Amanda will be here with you," I say.

"No!" she says, her eyes filling up with tears.

"Amanda loves you," I say.

"Don't go, Mama." Tears fall down her cheeks. I feel lousy for leaving her; at eighteen months, my little girl is already pretty dramatic and given to instant tears. I fall hard for them every time.

"Mama!" she cries.

She's still saying "Mama," which cracks me open inside. Give it another six months, and she'll say "Mommy." Seeing her grow up and away from me makes me sad. Still, right now, at this moment when I want to dash out of the house on a date I've been looking forward to, her growing up can't come fast enough.

"I'm not leaving for long," I tell her. "I'll be back."

Mae sucks harder. She'll be in good hands—no, she'll be in the *best* hands, with my best friend. Amanda is her true auntie here in New York, practically her second mom. Mae *loves* Amanda.

The doorbell rings.

"Sweetheart, it's time for me to go—"

"Don't go, Mama." She grabs both my breasts.

"Honey, I need to go."

"No, Mama!" She squeezes them like lemons; she's not letting go.

"Please, my baby girl."

She dives into my chest, sucking madly, moving back and forth between each breast.

Don't go, Mama.

It's probably just separation anxiety, perfectly normal for a child her age. I know, from all the parenting books I've read and the advice I've been given. Though this behavior is considered to be normal, I sometimes think she feels abandoned by her father. But that's probably me projecting all my worries and fears on to her—something I promised myself I would avoid.

Amanda goes into the hallway to buzz Victor into the building.

I want to yell out, "Tell him to go home!" What was I thinking? Trying to go on a date was a terrible idea. I haven't been on a date for over six months. And this is only my second date ever as a single mom.

I'm so used to being a mom—I don't know how to be a woman out on the town. I close my eyes and make crazy wishes. *Maybe he'll trip on the stairs and break his leg. Maybe he'll get stuck in the elevator on his way up.* Then I stop myself. *Alright, Rachel, snap out of this.* Here's a kind, sexy, interesting man I can talk to for a while and indulge in adult conversation. So what am I waiting for?

"You'll be just fine—" I say to Mae.

"No!" she cries. Her eyes are red.

Into this emotional scene walks Victor.

"Uh, hi," he says. "Hi," I say. My nipples are bright pink, like candy, still hanging out of my blouse. This is *not* how I imagined him seeing my breasts for the first time. Mae peers up at him but refuses to unhook her mouth from my chest.

"You remember Mae, don't you?" I ask, casting around for small talk and not succeeding.

He looks adorable in his 1970s bottle-green corduroys, jean jacket, and cowboy boots. His dark wavy hair is shiny and combed. He's only twenty-four—four years younger than I am—but he has such a mature air about him.

Amanda offers him a glass of water, and they wander into the kitchen, chatting about public school education.

Alone with Mae, I wonder, *How am I going to delatch my daughter?*

"One more sip from each side, okay?" I say to her.

"No!"

Maybe I should call the whole thing off. *Look, this was all a very big mistake,* I'd say to Victor. *You should just go home. You have no idea what you're getting yourself into here. You should leave now, before it's too late.*

But what am I getting into? I'm so used to the daily rhythms of motherhood—mashing baby food, reading nursery rhymes, going to bed by eight—that I don't know how to mingle with a man. My daughter is home base right now; this guy seems like an alien. I'm not sure if I'm capable of interacting with him.

Victor and Amanda come back into the living room and stand in the doorway. He's telling her how unpredictable his students can be: "No compasses are allowed in my class because they could be considered a weapon."

He sounds so *together*. He's only twenty-four and can handle a room of thirty-five aggressive teenagers. I can barely manage a baby girl. Sure, he can say goodbye to all those rowdy kids at the end of the day. I'm a mother day and night. There is not a break in this life called motherhood.

Still, I love being a mom. I could stay with Mae all night, cuddled up in Amanda's living room. Nursing her fulfills me. But I have to go, and I don't know how.

I pull my breast out of Mae's mouth. "It's going to be okay."

From the corner of the room, Victor clears his throat. This first date could not possibly be more awkward.

I stand up and try to back away. But Mae clasps my leg. "Mamaaaaaaaaaaa!"

Amanda moves in fast, lying down on the bed with Mae. She wraps her arms around Mae's little body, as tears stream down her cheeks. I stand up and button my blouse. I better get out of here before I burst into tears, too.

As Victor turns around to the door, Amanda motions to me. She's giving him the thumbs-up behind his back. She has *never* given any man I've dated the thumbs-up.

"Go," she whispers. "Have a great time."

When the elevator doors close, I still hear Mae crying.

"Are you okay?" Victor asks. He looks into my eyes.

"Sure, I'll be fine," I say, turning my face away from him.

I can hold it together on the surface. Later, I can curl into a ball, crying my eyes out. But not now. Right now I'm determined to have a good time. *This is a date, dammit. And I'm going to enjoy it.*

"You look lovely," Victor tells me in the elevator.

"Thanks," I say.

My jean skirt is snug around my ass. My long brown hair is parted on one side. I'm wearing pink lip gloss and silver hoop earrings. This is much different from my daily uniform of worn jeans, a sweatshirt, and no jewelry.

But I'm holding my breath. I wish he'd stop looking at me. I want to stop the elevator and jump out. I want to rush back upstairs and curl myself into Mae. I want Amanda to hold me, too. Why can't I just relax and enjoy my first date in a long time?

I glance at Victor. Just look at him. He's just a mere boy compared with me. Still, he's a math teacher, a man of numbers. I'm all about English and writing—the fact that we're so different intrigues me. I like his deep voice and the stubble around his cheeks. I think we look cute together. Still, right here in the elevator, I feel the pull of Mae; no matter what, we'll be fine, just the two of us. Think of all those strong, tight single-mother-and-daughter teams in those movies, *Tumbleweeds* and *Anywhere But Here,* which ironically I saw when I was pregnant. In *Tumbleweeds,* the very independent single mom (Janet McTeer) hits the road with her daughter after her life starts to turn sour. In *Anywhere But Here,* the mother (played by Susan Sarandon) leaves her second husband and heads for Beverly Hills with her daughter (Natalie Portman) to begin a new chapter. Oh yeah, but that's Hollywood, not real life.

By the time we get to the park, I've left the planet of mom.

I ask him about the new song lyrics he recorded in the studio last weekend. He asks me about editing kindergarten phonics books: "Is that really the best way to learn how to read?" He's not only cute, he's theoretical. I like that. I am truly happy to be out with him.

We find our seats, and the play begins. It's serious and somber: A gypsy mother travels with an army, scrounging for food. She's spiteful. She throws food at her children—"Eat!"—but ignores their other needs, their emotions. In the end, each child dies. Not exactly light fare for a summer evening.

As soon as I feel a chill in the air, Victor takes off his jacket and wraps it around my shoulders. I smile at him, grateful.

"How about a beer?" Victor asks as we leave the park.

"It's kind of late." My mind is running on one track right now: Mae.

"It's only ten o'clock," he says.

"That's late," I say.

"It is?"

I'm serious. Too serious. But as soon as I think, *This is a date, after all,* my mind bounces back to Mae. I'm a mother. I've got to get home.

We start walking back to the East Village in silence. When I glance over at him, I see his disappointment. The truth is, I do like him. He's sweet. He plays the guitar and writes music. He kind of looks like the actor Vin Diesel—only with hair. He has chiseled features and a smooth Southern accent. He uses slang from the eighties, like, "Oh, that's awesome."

But I'm torn. I still feel guilty about leaving Mae—and the play didn't help matters. As we walk, though, I start to reconsider: We've only been out for an hour and a half. What's the rush? Sure, I need my sleep, but it's only ten o'clock on a Friday. Mae will sleep soundly for a few hours. If I go home, I'll probably just sit there and stare at her. I remember dating advice I read this week, while I was skimming how-to books for single parents at Barnes & Noble (Mae was asleep in her sling): "You can be a lover and a mother," it said in the promisingly titled *Sex & the Single Parent: A Guide for Parents Who Find Themselves Back in the Dating Game.* "But you can't do it torn apart inside by guilt or uncertainty." Well, that really made me feel super. "You can only date if deep inside you can trust yourself to make the right decisions most of the time," the book went on. "The trick is going in a measured fashion." I didn't know there would be any tricks involved.

All right, maybe one little beer won't hurt.

We duck into a shadowy bar on First Avenue. When Victor orders, I notice his sideburns. How adorable. When we clink our bottles together, our eyes meet.

"Thanks for deciding to stay a little longer," he says.

"I'm glad I did."

I really am. Victor is gentle and polite, not a player like Mark the lawyer—or any of the men I ran around with pre-motherhood.

I like the way he looks, too: His mom is Brazilian, and his dad is white, so his skin is light brown, like Mae's. I like the fact that Victor looks like her. Before our first date is even over, I imagine us as a family. Yes, we could all fit together. She and I are a nontraditional family. Victor's skin color might make it easier to blend together into that nuclear family I want.

"So, tell me about your last girlfriend," I say to Victor.

"My last?"

"Yeah."

"There's not much to say," he tells me. "It was kind of short lived."

"I get it. Then tell me about the last woman you lived with."

"Lived with?" he says. "I've never lived with anyone. Actually, I've never had a serious relationship."

"You haven't?"

Here I am, already married and divorced. In the past ten years, I've lived with three men. I see a red flag waving around Victor's head right now. He's never been in a long-term relationship—*not* a good sign, although he *is* charming and cute.

But it's not like a red flag has stopped me before. Maybe this time it will be different. I'll be in charge. I'll call the shots. I'll take the lead—for once—and ask for what I really want.

But what *do* I want right now? Sex? Companionship? Love? All three? I want him to hold me. I want him to rub the small of my back. I want to rest my head on his shoulder. I want him to breathe me in and say, *Rachel, I could lie with you all night.* Pretty tall order when you think about it. Sometimes I want nothing; sometimes I want it all. Even I find it confusing.

We order another round of beers. He pulls out a pack of cigarettes, and I reach over to take one. I haven't had a cigarette for over two years, but it feels like it's time to just let go. When we leave the bar at midnight, Victor insists I wear his jacket. I'm tipsy, stumbling in the dark, as taxis zip past us. I look up at the lights in the buildings across the street and wonder what strangers are doing behind those windows. It gives me the feeling of possibility. As we cross the street, I reach out and take Victor's hand. He squeezes my fingers.

Outside Amanda's building, we reach for each other, a brief hug. But all at once, I'm not ready for this to end. I want more.

"Do you want to come upstairs?" I ask.

"Upstairs?" he says. "But your daughter is there, and your friend."

"Just walk me to the door," I say.

I pull out my keys and unlock the front door. Victor and I ride the elevator up timidly, standing inches apart from each other. When we step out, the bright lights shine against the linoleum. It's like sunshine, too intense. I touch Victor's arm and he pulls me to him.

"Close your eyes," I say.

I bury my face in his shoulder, and he kisses the side of my head. I reach up and touch his face. Heaven.

Victor slides right into our life, as if we've been together forever, when in fact it's been only three weeks. This has always been my pattern: to connect with a man and tuck him right under my wing. C'mon, who doesn't love to fall in love? I've always found that place with a man—where we stand closely, looking into each other's eyes, longing, willing to take it to the next level—irresistible.

This evening, he's wearing my red checkered apron, stirring up sweet potatoes and collard greens at the stove. The brown rice is steaming, and we're drinking Czech beer. Mae is painting at an easel near the window. It's a nice family tableau, and I think, *Hey, I could get used to this.*

"You have no idea how good that smells," I say, touching his arm.

Victor made the same dish last weekend, and I asked for it again because it is so tasty. Just to have a man cooking in my kitchen makes me happy. "The reason you love this dish so much is that it's a mix of the sweet with the bitter," he says.

The sweet with the bitter.

"So, that's your secret," I say, reaching out to hug him. He kisses my cheek. I breathe in the basil on his lips. I can't believe that we met just three weeks ago. I'm falling hard for him.

"You're so good to me," I say.

But Mae drops her paintbrush and rushes up, clinging to my leg.

"In the middle!" she says, pushing us apart. She wants to be right there, sandwiched between us. I lift her up; Victor and I hold on to her, the three of us connected.

"You're the jelly," Victor says. We all laugh.

It's time to eat, and Mae sits in my lap at the table. Victor feeds her bits of sweet potato.

"*Mmmmm,*" he says, dipping the spoon to her lips.

She claps her hands. "Sing!" she says. At just one and a half, she's already very talkative.

Victor has a lovely, deep voice and his strong Southern accent is a big turn-on. I'm charmed by the songs he makes up for Mae on the spot. "Oh, my little Mae, my darling . . . " He has a great comfort level with her. She doesn't freak him out.

After dinner, I nurse Mae to sleep in our bed while Victor washes the dishes. When I tiptoe back out, he's writing next week's lesson plans for his math class. I kiss the back of his neck, and he stands up to wrap his arms around me. We move over to the sofa bed and fall into each other. "Go to sleep, sweetie," he says, stroking my hair.

I sigh and close my eyes. "That's it," he says, kissing my forehead. "You're beautiful when you sleep."

I'm exhausted, and he seems to understand this. He holds me close, without any expectation of sex. Sleeping with Victor is a world apart from my one-night stand with Mark. Victor simply embraces me as if I'm a precious package.

The next morning, Mae and Victor cuddle up together on the sofa bed and watch *Sesame Street.* She drapes her legs over his. I make hot cocoa for them.

"Did you know that Grover has a single mom?" Victor asks me.

"Really?" I say

"Yeah, take a seat," he says, patting the mattress. "You'll see."

I think back to all the episodes of *Sesame Street* I've watched. He's right: I don't remember Grover having a father. It's just him and his single mom—see, he turned out just fine. All of a sudden, I have a real fondness for Grover.

We pack a picnic for our trip to Wave Hill, a twenty-eight-acre public garden on the Hudson River in the Bronx. A short bus ride from Washington Heights, the estate was deeded to the public in the 1960s. Mark Twain lived there for a few years in the early 1900s. His description of spending winter there sums up why this place is my sanctuary:

I believe we have the noblest roaring blasts here I have ever known on land; they sing their hoarse song through the big tree-tops with a splendid energy that thrills me and stirs me and uplifts me and makes me want to live always.

We ride the bus uptown, and walk the half mile to the gardens. Mae falls asleep in the pack on my back. Her head, kept warm with a rainbow-colored knit hat, bobs up and down on my shoulder with every step I take.

"You're so awesome," Victor tells me as we go through the gates.

"Thanks," I say. "You are, too."

"No, really," he says. "You're beautiful. You're real. And you're sexy."

I tug on his arm, and pull him close. I want to haul him into me. I want him to be a part of me. Mae is awake now. When she sees that we're here, she wants to get down. She shrieks in joy, toddling in front of us. Even in the winter, I love the way the bare trees billow over us.

"Chase me!" Mae yells.

Victor runs after her, trying to catch her shadow. They're a silly pair and have so much fun. I'm the serious one. I'm the one who's always thinking, always worrying about Mae, and our future. I'm in awe of how companionable they are. We walk over to our favorite place here, the garden pool where water lilies and lotus grow. Orange koi hide in the plants' roots. Mae bends over the water, close to the edge, looking down.

"Fishies?" she says. "Little fishies?"

Victor holds her waist so she won't fall in.

"There's one," Victor says, pointing to a huge koi, its gills sparkling beneath the surface.

"Fishy!" she screams.

I stand behind Victor and hold on to his arms. When I bend forward, I see our reflection in the water, the three of us holding each other up. Mae points to the water. "Daddy," she says.

No one says a word.

She still points right at Victor's reflection. "Daddy," she says.

No one corrects her.

Later, Victor gets ready to go back to Brooklyn. He's teaching at 8 AM tomorrow. I also have an editing deadline tonight.

After Mae goes to sleep, I ask him about what happened today. "That was kind of intense," I say, "when she called you 'Daddy.'"

"You're not kidding," he says.

"How did you feel when she said that?" I ask.

"Like an imposter."

"Why?"

"It doesn't seem right. How can I take responsibility for something that I had no part in?"

"But are you okay with it?"

"Yes," he whispers, holding on to my waist.

I relax into him. I don't say anything else, but somehow, this all feels so natural. She's not just *my* baby anymore. She's becoming *our* baby.

Here I go, wanting to have the perfect family—even though we've known each other only three weeks. But it's so easy to make Victor the daddy after such a short time.

The next morning, at 6 AM, Mae runs into the living room. "Daddy?"

"Victor had to go home, honey."

"I want Daddy!" she says.

"I'm sorry."

"I want Daddy!" she stomps her feet. Tears fall down her cheeks. She loves him, too. Already. This is sweet and heartbreaking. I pick Mae up and hold her in my arms. "You miss him, don't you?"

She sniffles.

"He'll be back soon," I say, although I feel bad because I can't really make these kinds of promises to her.

The next night, as if on cue, Eric calls. Can he somehow sense that another man might be encroaching on his territory?

The phone rings. I don't have Caller ID.

"How are my girls?" a deep voice says.

It's Eric. I hold my breath.

"Rachel?" he says. "I'm worried about you two."

"Why?" I ask. *Why the hell is he calling me now, a whole year later?*

"I'm coming back," Eric says. "After September 11, things aren't the same."

"You're coming back from where?"

"Europe."

"Where in Europe?" I ask.

"It doesn't matter."

"When?"

I'm rattling off questions, although I don't really believe he'll come back, after so long. *He can't come back. I've just met someone, I'm falling in love. He can't do this to me.*

"I love you, Rach," he says.

I choke inside. "You're missing out, Eric," I say. "You're missing out on her whole life."

He is Mae's father. He's the man I decided to have a baby with. He's also everything familiar, no matter how foolish and irrational that sounds.

"I don't want to miss out anymore," Eric says.

I don't want him to hear me crying. I don't want him to see my tears falling. I don't want him to know how his voice still strikes me down.

"I'll be there soon."

"Soon?" *Why is he doing this to me? It's not fair.*

"I don't have a ticket yet."

He's lying. I should just hang up the phone. *Hang up right now.* The grownup in me knows what to do. *Just hang up the damn phone. Hang up on him. What are you waiting for? Go now. Get on with your life.*

He's already missed so much: when Mae said her first sentence, when she took her first steps, when she blew out her first birthday candles. There's no way to go back.

"Baby, I have to come back," he says. "I have to see you. I have to see Mae."

"I know," I say and sigh. In that moment, I know I want him back. Even though I've made great strides in my life, the sound of his voice makes me feel like I haven't moved forward at all. In fact, I move backward. I return to a place I don't want to be, but I can't help inhabiting.

When I see Victor on Friday, I'm on edge. Mae was up four times the night before to nurse. My nipples are sore. My neck is so stiff I can't turn my head to the right. Eric's voice keeps running through my head. Should I tell Victor that he's been calling? Why should I make a big deal of something that's not even real?

Tonight, Victor opens his backpack and pulls out a few men's dress shirts.

"Here," he says, handing them to me. "They're a little small for me, and I'd like you to have them."

I'm touched. He's asking me to wear *him*. *Does this mean that I can finally throw out Eric's clothes?*

Mae comes over and grabs one of the shirts. "Mine!" she says. She tries to pull Victor's shirt over her head, but it gets stuck. We laugh.

"Help!" she says.

I pull the shirt off her head, and Victor lifts her up. He throws her in the air, her feet dangling. She giggles. He's tireless.

I want a family so badly right now that I'm willing to think that this man—who I've been dating for barely one month— could be the One.

Just after Thanksgiving—exactly one year after Eric split town— our lobby buzzer rings. It's 10 AM, and I'm editing a textbook. Mae is with Amanda at the playground. I'm not expecting anyone.

I push the TALK button. "Yes? Who is it?"

"Eric."

Holy shit.

"Let me up, Rach."

"No," I say. How did he find out where I live? His sister, most likely.

"Please, Rach, let me up."

"No," I say. "I'll come down."

My hands are shaking, and I can feel the adrenaline course through my system. Where's my jacket? Should I pull my hair back? I'm not thinking straight. I should call a girlfriend. Amanda wouldn't allow him in here over her dead body. I should go to my neighbors, who've heard enough about Eric to barricade the door. Although I've spent countless hours—especially after he first left—dreaming of this moment, I feel totally unable to process the fact that he's downstairs. And though I know I should stand firm and refuse to see him, another part of me is not giving up so easily. It's simple: I'm thinking with my heart when I should be thinking with my head.

Which explains why I grab my sweatshirt and race downstairs.

"You got so skinny," Eric says to me. He's leaning against the light post.

"Thanks. You got fat," I say, with only a little sarcasm in my voice.

He now has a belly. His face is bloated and pasty. He's probably gained at least ten pounds.

"That's because I quit smoking," he says.

"Good for you," I say. "How long has it been?"

"Three months."

"Impressive, Eric. I'm glad you're taking care of yourself."

We're like two old friends, chatting on a brisk morning on a Manhattan street corner. If you passed us, you'd never guess that this guy abandoned his baby girl and me a year ago. You'd never know that he hasn't been back since that day. I'm so anxious and nervous and pissed off yet glad to see him that it throws me off.

He reaches out and touches my waist. I flinch. "Here's your stuff," he says, handing me a black duffel bag.

"My stuff?"

I unzip the bag and see my old ratty bathrobe, a handful of CDs, and a book by James Baldwin that once belonged to me. He'd taken these things a year ago when he split town. I never missed them.

"Thanks," I say. "I guess."

Why would he return these things now? *What the fuck are you doing here?* I want to scream.

But the calm wins out and my anger continues to boil under the surface.

"Let's walk," I say.

I want to keep moving, to keep from exploding. We head over to the flower gardens at 190th Street and find a green park bench that faces the garden. I sit inches away from him, not touching.

I want to stand my ground. I have a right to know where he's been for a year—and more important, why he left.

"I missed you, Rach." He reaches out and puts his hand on my knee.

I freeze, and I say nothing. His palm rests on my kneecap, warm and familiar. My fingers tingle, thrilled, but my legs are tense. I should get up and walk away, now. I know this is wrong.

"Why did you leave?" I ask, barely able to keep from screaming.

He shrugs, like it doesn't matter. Like it's entirely natural to leave your girlfriend and baby one day without warning and to not return.

"Where did you go?" I ask. "What have you been doing?"

"Does it matter now?" he says. "I'm back now, aren't I?" He leans over and lets his head fall down. He looks like he hasn't slept in days.

In a perverse way, he's right. What does it matter? Even if I had some answers, what good would it do? But I feel like I need to know. After a year of wondering what went wrong, I'm more than a little entitled to some answers.

"Did you leave me for another woman?" I ask. I always thought this might be it. I deserve to know.

"No, Rach. I had a nervous breakdown."

"Did you check yourself into a mental hospital?" Before he left, he'd talked about this, he'd said that his head was so fucked up that he didn't know what to do. I wish this was the truth—that he had a mental breakdown and went to a hospital—but I know it's not. It's just his excuse for leaving like he did.

He shakes his head. "I've got to see my baby. She's not home?"

"No," I say. I'm not going to tell him that Mae is two blocks from here, at the playground up the street. I feel like the mama bear that will attack him if he gets too close to her cub.

"I've got to see her," he says. He lifts his head and looks at me with his bloodshot eyes.

"Then you need to do some things first," I say.

"Here we go," he huffs. "What?"

"First, you need to pay me back the $3,000 you stole from my bank account the day before you left."

"Sure, Rach," he says in a mocking voice.

"What's that supposed to mean?" I say.

"I'll pay you back, but I don't have all the money right now"

"Fine then, start with $100 a week," I say.

"I'm looking for a job."

"Then find one," I counter. I'm proud of myself for telling him what I really think, instead of backing off or making excuses for him. He owes me money. He lied to me. He's irresponsible and unreliable.

After Mae was born, I tried to shield her from Eric. His alcoholism was full-blown by that time—biweekly trips to the bar, stumbling in at 3 AM. He was either drunk or hungover; I didn't want him alone with Mae during the day. I was a nervous wreck of a mother, hovering over her. When he took her, she cried. It made me frantic, and I pulled her away. She was always my greatest concern—and I'll never be sorry for that.

"Please let me see Mae," he says. "Please."

"Not yet."

"I'm her father," he says.

I nod my head. He *is* her father. He will always be her father. There's no way I can go back and change that. But is that grounds enough to let him see her? I'm not feeling sorry for Eric, and I certainly won't allow him to see Mae unless I'm right by her side.

"I'm sorry, Rach," he says. "I've got to see my baby." His voice cracks. "I'm sorry, I'm so sorry." He's crying now, the tears running down his cheeks.

What bullshit.

I don't believe him. This is just an act. He's always been a good actor. But he won't stop crying. A couple walks by, and he sniffles loudly, no doubt for attention. The woman turns her head, concerned.

I take a deep breath, ready to get up and leave him and all the misery he's brought me, here on the park bench. But his tears are breaking through my hard shield. Here's that sensitive, intense man I fell in love with, the man who felt things so deeply he didn't sleep at night. Every day, he remembered his mom who died too early, and his tough, sometimes violent childhood in the Bronx. The pain I've felt since he left suddenly seems like a dream—and I'm trying hard to keep myself firmly anchored in reality. But I'm slipping.

"Can I have a hug?" Eric says. I look at his wet cheeks. *No. Don't do it.* I hold my breath and try to hold still like a statue. *You can't touch me. You can't get inside me, I'm so solid.* Eric stands up and reaches out to me. I stare at his long brown fingers.

Don't, Rachel. Don't do it. This is the grownup in me talking. She's clear-headed and conscious. She knows that if he touches me, I'll weaken. The grownup in me knows that I can contain all this grief and anger. She says, *Hold on to yourself, girl.*

Eric puts his hand on my shoulder. "Come here," he whispers. "Let me hold you." He hasn't forgotten how much I love to be held by him. But I also know how manipulative he can be. And I know this tactic has worked when I hear myself say, "Okay." I stand up and practically fall into his six-foot-tall frame, as he embraces me, his long arms wrapped around my back.

I rest my head on his chest and breathe him in. He smells clean, not like the tobacco-Eric I remember. We stand there for a long minute before I pull away. He's stopped crying. I know this was all a bad idea, but I couldn't help myself.

A few hours later, I'm still going through all the pros and cons about Eric: Sure, he's Mae's father, but can I count on him? Sure, he's blood, but how do I know if he'll stick around this time? That's when I remember Victor is coming over tonight for dinner.

I resolve not to tell him what happened today. I feel too guilty about the hug, but more so about the fragility of our new relationship. I need to protect it. "Eric's back," I could say. But Victor will ask if I've talked to him or seen him. If it were me, I'd be the same way.

I've been crying off and on all afternoon, and I'm an awful liar.

When Victor shows up that evening, he leans over and kisses me. His stubble rubs against my cheek. He's wearing beige corduroy pants and cowboy boots. My cutie-pie.

"You okay, sweetheart?" he asks. He looks into my swollen eyes.

"Not really."

He reaches out and touches my arm. "Tell me what's going on."

"Daddy!" Mae says. She flies in from the bedroom, having heard his voice.

Not exactly, I think.

"Later," I whisper to him. "I'll tell you later, okay?"

Victor throws her in the air. She giggles. He is such a loving and goofy guy. It's funny and touching to hear her call him "Daddy." But now her real father is back. This is crazy. What am I going to do? Why did Eric have to come back now and ruin everything?

We sit down for pasta, salad, and beer. Mae sits on Victor's lap and eats noodles with her fingers.

"I want you to come to North Carolina with me this Christmas," Victor says.

"North Carolina?" I say. "With you? Both of us?"

"Of course," he says, rubbing his fingers through Mae's soft curls.

"That's so sweet of you." I swallow hard. "Have you asked your family?"

"Of course," he says. "My mom is really excited to meet you."

Yes, I think. This is the perfect plan. I can make my getaway. I'll fall in love, for real, with Victor. When I get back, Eric will be history.

If only it were that easy. It's so tempting, but it's also too easy. I know I can't run away from my life even though I want to.

After getting Mae to sleep, I find Victor lying on the sofa, reading. I'm hoping that he's forgotten about what I have to tell him. But he sits up. "Come here," he says, patting the spot next to him.

"Eric's back in town," I say, biting my lip. I tell him about our meeting today, how Eric wants to see Mae and I'm not sure what to do.

"Do you still have feelings for him?" Victor asks.

"No!"

"Are you sure?"

"I'm confused," I say.

"Confused?"

"I'm falling hard for you," I say. "I wish Eric hadn't come back."

"So, don't see him."

"I know," I say. "But it's not that easy. This is her father."

Victor turns his head away from me.

"Please," I say.

"I have a bad feeling about this."

"We'll go with you for Christmas, and it will all work out," I say.

"I can't stay here tonight," he says. "It doesn't feel right."

"Don't do this," I say.

But he gets up in silence, puts his coat on, and walks out the door.

The week before Christmas, Mae and I are supposed to meet Eric in the children's book section at Barnes & Noble at Columbus

Circle at noon. She tugs a *Sesame Street* touch-and-feel book off the shelf and hands it to me.

"Read, *puhleeze*," she says.

I pull her into my lap and glance at my watch. Eric is late. Am I surprised? No.

I've agreed to let him see her before we take off on our holiday trip. I told Victor about my plan to see Eric again; although he seemed hurt, I decide to go through with it anyway.

Eric has been calling me at least three times a day, begging me to change my mind and let him see Mae just once. At first, I stand my ground. Then one evening, he shows up with $200 worth of groceries from Whole Foods. He remembers all my favorite foods, of course, like tempeh, sharp cheese, and fresh bread. When Eric wants something, he'll do anything to get it. He's trying to win me over.

For days, I worry about how to explain to Mae that we are going to see Eric. She's only twenty months old. Would she even remember him? Of course not.

As Mae ate oatmeal this morning, I propped her in front of the TV and turned on a video of her at three months old. In it, Eric blows raspberries inches away from her face. "Little Munch," he is saying. "Oh, my Little Munch." This was his nickname for her when I was pregnant: During my one and only ultrasound, she was puckering her lips as if she were munching. The name stuck.

"This is you," I said to Mae, pointing to the screen as if I'm her third grade teacher giving a supplemental lesson. I realized I was doing this for me—and not for her. After all, she's way too young to remember Eric.

"And this is Eric," I said.

She was nonchalant, not paying attention.

"Do you know who Eric is?" I asked.

She shook her head. Eric meant nothing to her.

"This is Eric," I tried again. "He's your father."

Still, Mae said nothing. I thought, *This was all a very bad idea.*

"Eric helped me make you," I said. "He left for a while. But now he's back."

"Turn it off," Mae said.

"We're going to see Eric today," I said, ignoring her. "He's come back to see you."

"I want Elmo," Mae said, dropping her spoon on the table.

In the bookstore now, she reaches out her hand and touches Elmo on the cover.

"Elmo," she says. "I love you, Elmo."

I glance down at my watch. Eric is fifteen minutes late. My palms are sweaty.

"Elmo is red," Mae says.

I've stopped reading. She's taken over for me.

"Elmo is soft," she says.

"Hi, girls," says a deep voice behind us.

I jump to my feet, pulling Mae into my arms. Her book falls to the floor.

"Elmo!" she cries.

"Hi, Eric," I say.

I'm gripping Mae, protecting her. I'm afraid that he might reach out and touch her, that he might scare her.

"Mae, this is your father, Eric."

"Hi, my baby," he says, coming closer.

Her little body tightens in my arms. Her eyes are glued to the floor, to her book. "Elmo?" she asks.

"Mae, can you please say 'Hi'?" I ask her.

"No!"

She squirms in my arms. "Elmo," she says. "I want Elmo."

I let her down, and she retrieves her book. Eric stands there, not saying anything.

"Read, Mama," Mae says, handing me the book. I sit down again, and take her into my lap.

"Elmo loves the winter," I say. "It's cold and snowy. Everyone bundles up."

Eric crouches down next to us. He's close but not touching. Mae keeps her eyes on Elmo. After the last page, she jumps off my knees and walks away. She strolls through the aisles, pointing to the animals on one book cover. "Kitty says *meow*," she says. "Doggy says *woof-woof.*"

I stay right beside her, as Eric straggles behind.

She spots a little yellow stuffed duck and grabs it. "Oh, my baby duckie," she says, rocking it in her arms.

"She's mad at me," he says.

"Maybe," I say. *Let him feel guilty. Let him see that his own daughter doesn't remember him.*

Mae keeps walking, she's the leader now. I stay close to her.

"Come, Mama," she says, leading me over to the pop-up books. Eric stays close behind me, this tall African American man following us around the bookstore. He ambles behind us, but we have no connection. He could be a stranger. Or a stalker.

"Are you girls hungry?" Eric asks. "I'll get you a pretzel in the park."

"Pretzel!" Mae says.

"Sure, why not?" I say. Here he is, showing up a year later, penniless, and he's going to buy us a pretzel. I made a silent vow to myself last night that we'd spend two hours with him, that's it. Two hours will be plenty of time. We've been in the bookstore for only twenty minutes.

"Mae loves the merry-go-round in Central Park," I say. "We can head that way." I want to stay in charge here.

"Merry-go-round!" she shrieks.

I pull on her pink winter jacket, and Eric tugs her hat over her ears.

"Eric," Mae says, pointing at him.

"That's Dad to you," he says, touching her cheek.

"Eric," she says again.

He looks upset. "Did you do this?" he asks me.

"Do what?"

"Tell her to call me Eric."

"C'mon now," I say. "She's calling you Eric because I call you Eric. She doesn't know who you are. She doesn't remember you."

There, I've said it. *She does not remember you.*

We step out into the cold air and head for the park. I'm carrying Mae on my hip. Without a word, Eric takes the heavy backpack from me—filled with crackers, a banana, a water bottle, cloth diapers—and straps it on his shoulders. As we head down 66th Street, he reaches out and touches Mae's long slender fingers.

"Oh, baby, your hands are cold," he says. "You need some gloves."

Sure enough, we see a man with a little cart, filled with knitted hats and scarves—and gloves. Eric bolts ahead and looks at the tiniest pairs. When we reach him, he's holding up two colors.

"Which ones?" he asks me.

"Red," Mae answers.

Of course, red, her favorite color, like Elmo. He pays and slips the gloves over Mae's fingers, squeezing her little thumbs into the right place.

This moment is exactly how I'd envisioned our family, out together for an afternoon stroll in the winter, with Daddy buying a pair of new gloves for his little girl, the three of us sweet and loving and forever true. This is the moment I've wanted, always. But it's not so sweet, not so charming. A year later won't cut it, nor should it.

"You sure got your nana's long, slender fingers," he says, referring to his mother, Mae's namesake, who died over a decade ago.

"You were named after your nana, too," I say to Mae. I know this means nothing to her now—the fact that she's named for Eric's mother. I'm probably just saying it to rub in the guilt.

Before we reach the carousel, Mae hears the music. "Merry-go-round!" she says. She wants to get down and walk. She wants to move faster, to lead. She toddles in front of us.

"I have a boyfriend," I tell Eric.

He pauses midstep. "I'm not surprised."

"We're going away for Christmas together," I say. "With Mae."

Eric says nothing. We walk the rest of the way in silence. At the ticket booth, he purchases three tickets and lifts Mae onto a big horse with sparkling jewels. He stands on one side of the horse, holding her leg, and I stand on the other side.

Being on separate sides of Mae is the way it has to be. We're on separate horses now.

If the bumpy plane ride to North Carolina is any indication of where my relationship with Victor is going, things are not proceeding smoothly. It's supposed to be a smooth, easy, two-hour flight. But suddenly, things turn turbulent. The plane cuts sharply to the right. I grip Mae in my lap.

"We've hit a rough patch," the pilot announces.

"Shit," Victor whispers.

The plane bucks into the air again and we rise off our seats, airborne.

"Fuck," Victor says, *not* in a whisper.

I stop breathing. I clutch Mae and pray, *Please let us live.*

I've heard that traveling together is a true test of a new relationship. We're heading south for ten days. I'm going to meet

Victor's family: his mom and dad, big brother, aunts and uncles, cousins. I feel like we've been together for years—but it's only been two months. Is all this happening too fast? Maybe I should be putting the brakes on. Instead, in my suitcase are beautiful black-and-white photos I took of Victor and Mae, his arms wrapped around her on a cold afternoon outside our apartment. I've framed them as Christmas gifts for his whole family. *What am I doing?*

"Everyone stay seated, *please*," the pilot says.

"Shit," Victor says again, his face white.

"We do have little ears around here," I say under my breath.

"Sorry."

"Please hold my hand," I ask him, reaching across his lap and grabbing his.

The plane swoops in the air again.

"Fuck," Victor says. He's losing it. Why can't he just pull it together? Granted, I'm used to being strong, but I can't take care of one more person here. I've got Mae, I can't baby him, too.

Get us down safely, I pray to a god I've never believed in.

Ironically, Mae, at a year and a half, is the heroic one. Every time the plane plunges, she laughs. "Again!" she says. The plane jumps and she giggles. "Again!"

The passengers behind us burst into nervous laughter. Victor's fingers are limp in my hand. I squeeze them, but there's no response. His eyes are closed. For a second, I wonder if he's fainting. *Why do I have to hold it together for all of us? When is it my turn to fall apart?*

"I need you to be strong right now," I say.

"I'm scared," he says.

"I am, too. But can't you try to stay calm?"

"No," he says.

"You're not helping—"

"Rachel, this might be the end."

"Stop," I say. "I'm asking you to be tough right now. You're going to be fine." My voice is high pitched and squeaky; I'm terrified, too. But at least I'm putting on a good front. In fairness to Victor, when I get scared I also get unreasonable. In a tense situation, I can be difficult to deal with.

One long and terrifying hour later, there's a bumpy landing and a communal sigh. We're alive.

When we arrive in Raleigh at 10 PM, Victor's mother, a gorgeous Brazilian, is waiting for us. There's warm food on the stove.

"Thank you so much for coming," she says, giving me a hug. Then she whispers in my ear: "You're the first girlfriend he's ever introduced us to."

I stop breathing. *The first one? But that's impossible.*

After putting Mae to bed, I pull Victor into the hallway.

"We have to talk," I whisper. "Your mom just told me that I'm the first girlfriend she's ever met."

He nods his head yes.

"This is a joke, right?" I ask.

"No."

"But you're twenty-four," I say.

He shakes his head. "I've never been this serious about anyone."

Are we that serious? Suddenly, I'm not sure.

As the days pass, the head cold I arrived with only gets worse. I'm sick and cranky and feeling our differences like never before. He likes to smoke pot, something I wasn't aware of before. When his old high school buddies come over at night, they sit out back getting high. I can hear them laughing as I nurse my little girl to sleep in the twin bed we're sharing.

One evening, I make a pot of macaroni and cheese—Mae's favorite food—and as I'm feeding her, Victor walks in and starts eating from the pot with a spoon.

"This hits the spot," he says. I wonder if he's high again. He doesn't ask if Mae wants more. He keeps eating, and within minutes, the pot is empty.

"How thoughtless," I say to him. I'm at the sink, banging dishes together under hot running water. Just look at me now, the tight-assed older woman muttering under her breath in the kitchen.

"Excuse me?" he says.

"You could have asked if we wanted more before gobbling it all up," I explain, trying to be more reasonable.

"I'm sorry," he says.

"Sure you are," I say. So much for reasonable.

He looks like an oversized little boy. He stands at the sink, holding out a cheesy spoon, like a gobbled up lollipop. Even though I'm just a few years older than he, I feel like we're generations apart. I have a child. I have years of relationship experiences. I admit, those relationships were something I hope my daughter never models. But all the drama I've been through with men pushed me to grow up.

Still, I've never played this role before: the Older Woman.

Every time I glance over at him, I think, *Aw, he's so cute.* Taking care of others has always come easily for me. Maybe it's because I'm a Cancer—I thrive on cooking, serving hot meals, healing wounds. I like being the one in charge, the one who calls all the shots. Yes, this kind of control suits me—in a way.

But maybe Victor needs some time to grow up. Is he dad-material? *Hmmm,* probably not. At least not yet.

As the days pass, I notice that Victor is rebelling in different ways. He sleeps in every morning; Mae and I wake up at daybreak and wait for him to get up. His high school buddies drop by every night at Mae's bedtime. Victor gives me a peck on the cheek and wanders outside to smoke pot. I hear them huddling in the snow with a pipe. Why didn't I know about his pot smoking before? Is he regressing?

More to the point, do I blame him? We're probably just reinforcing each other's bad behavior. We're snapping a lot at each other. This is not good.

I climb into bed with Mae and nurse her, the two of us tucked into one tight twist. At 2 AM, I hear Victor come in the front door. I'm sure he's high. He goes into his room to sleep. I don't get up and join him. We haven't had sex for five days, but that's actually okay, considering I'm premenstrual, moody, and pissed off.

I lie awake and think about Eric. I wonder if there's any chance of patching things up. A future with him is futile, I know that. Why can't I just see him as my sperm donor and move on? I'm obsessing. He always used to say that I was his "Shelter from the Storm," like the Bob Dylan song. In my mind, the three of us are back together, a family again. It's often said that the definition of insanity is doing the same thing over and over and expecting different results. Don't ask me how I get it into my head that Eric is just waiting to whisk us away into a story with a happy ending. Maybe I read too many fairytales as a kid. I'd be the perfect candidate for that reality show, *The Bachelorette.* Just give me my handsome man and surely he'll take me off to his countryside villa to live in bliss. What's the matter with me?

What I really can't get out of my head is the fact that Eric and Mae are connected by blood. We're supposed to be a nuclear family. I don't want Mae to have a stepfather; she deserves to be raised by the parents she comes from, like a plant from the same genus. We're all flesh and blood, a tribe. *There I go again, believing the fairytale.*

I'm hanging on to the phantom of Eric, like a ghost in my closet, always there. I wish I could change him somehow. I wish he'd stop drinking, that he'd pay the bills. I wish I could make things right for Mae somehow. She's *supposed* to have a dad.

Could I have done things differently? Of course. I criticized Eric for holding Mae the wrong way and burping her too hard. I didn't let him spend enough time with her. But if I'd done things differently, would he have stuck around? I don't know.

Ours is the family that wouldn't happen, no matter how much I wanted it.

I wish I could push Eric out of my head, make him disappear. I *could* be with another man. Can't I see that going back to Eric is going to lead only to more heartbreak? Obviously not.

I thought I was falling in love with Victor, but now Eric is back, and I have to give him one last go. There's a huge hole in my heart, overflowing with anxiety and sadness, and I can't contain it anymore. (And I haven't yet met my two best single-mom friends, Siobhan and Arden. It's Siobhan who will say to me a year later, "Don't go back for more where there is only less." *Don't go back for more where there is only less.* "If only I'd known you in New York," I will tell her. "I needed to hear that a year ago.")

So, when Christmas Eve rolls around, Victor is hanging out at a local bar with friends. I put Mae to bed and sneak into Victor's bedroom to use the phone. I dial Eric's sister's number in Harlem where Eric is staying. When the answering machine picks up, I pound the phone back into the receiver.

My fingers are shaking. *What the hell are you doing?* I should call someone else instead. I should dial Amanda in the East Village and say, "I'm having a hard time." I should call my sister and cry, or even one of my male friends, like Raul.

I'd already confessed to Amanda that I'd gone to the bookstore with Mae to meet Eric. She disapproved. "Rachel! What are you doing? Not only did he leave you, but he stole money from you."

"I know, but—"

"He's disturbed," she told me. "There's something mentally wrong with him."

"But he's still Mae's father," I said, feeling defensive.

"You seemed to be making a lot of progress. You were really getting on your feet again. I'm not so sure now."

I said nothing.

"You've got to think about Mae, too," she said. "This could really damage her."

Why do I have to know if Eric still loves me? Why? I'm a romantic and an optimist—a lethal combination. Right now, my idealism is kicking in. I've been on the dating treadmill for only a short time. I don't like it. I want to get off. Things with Victor aren't meant to be. Eric and I had conceived Mae in love and with hope. Why can't my fairytale come true?

I sit on the edge of Victor's bed and wrap my arms around myself. I'm bursting with so much anger and sadness that I feel like I'm about to explode. I don't know how to hold myself. I don't know how to be still with my feelings.

I lift the phone and dial again. Eric picks up.

"I'm down south with my boyfriend," I say. "But I'm coming home early."

"Alone?" he asks.

"Yes. Just me and Mae."

"That's good," he says.

The next morning, on Christmas, Victor doesn't have presents for me or for Mae. He simply forgot, he says. I'm a sucker for gifts—especially when it comes to my daughter. I feel like I have to give him instructions for everything, or he just doesn't get it.

But to be fair, maybe I'm just finding fault in everything he does. I'm looking for a way out. I want to go home.

That night, I go into his room and wake him up.

"I'm sorry, but we're leaving early," I say.

"Huh?"

"We're leaving tomorrow morning," I say. "I can't stay here, I'm sorry."

I'd called the airlines to change our tickets. Mae and I will take a 6 AM flight back to New York.

With no one to pick us up at LaGuardia, I take an expensive cab ride back to Washington Heights and carry a sleeping Mae in my arms upstairs. I slip her onto our bed. She'll be taking a long afternoon nap. But I'm wired. I'm alone, no one knows I'm back. The smart thing to do would be to call Amanda.

But I'm going to make the wrong choice. I know it. I pick up the phone and call Eric.

"We're back," I say.

"You are?"

"We came back this morning." My voice is breathy and frantic.

"Are you okay?"

"No," I say.

"Talk to me, Rach," he says. "Did that guy do something to you?"

"No," I say. "Of course not. We're fine. Just come over."

Why did I say, "Come over"? I said it without thinking. *I can take it back. I really can.*

"I'm coming," he says.

No, I'm *not* taking it back. I want him to come over. I know nothing good will come of it, but I still hope against hope.

Twenty minutes later, Eric is at my door. When he walks into my living room, I smell him. It's a smell I remember well, all man, like worn leather and sawdust. I want to fall into him and be caught in his earthiness. I want to feel steadied by him, by his ground, and taste the salt on his neck. I'm still so attracted to him—it's chemical—and I want him.

I still think that I can change things, make things right. I'll do this for Mae. And I'll do it for me. I'm not thinking about how painful this might be in the end, or the fact that you can't change someone who doesn't want to be changed. I know I must be out of my mind, but for now I don't care.

We stand inches away from each other in the middle of my living room, without talking. I so crave him and our old, familiar connection. I feel myself get warm between my legs. He reaches out now and wraps his arms around me. I smell beer on his breath but I choose to ignore it. This is the most perfect moment, being held like this.

"I love you," he says.

I say nothing.

He looks into my eyes. "I love you, Rach."

We are two shadows in the dark. The living room is barely lit by the lightbulb above the kitchen stove.

Let's do this one more time, I think. *Then he'll go, and we'll never see each other again.*

He reaches out and holds my hand. He leads me over to the sofa. He kisses me, his full lips on mine. I taste the alcohol he must have been drinking all night. I hear him undo his pants. I slide out of my sweatpants.

"You're so thin," he says.

He hasn't seen my body for over a year, when I still had all that baby weight.

I reach down to hold his cock. But he's soft. I gently stroke him. Nothing happens.

"Are you okay?" I ask.

"Yeah."

He spreads my legs apart and kisses my lips. I sigh.

"You're so wet," he says.

I reach down again and feel him, still limp. Why can't he get hard?

I want to feel him inside me one last time. Just one more time, and I won't go back. I know that he will not stop drinking, that he will continue to spiral downward.

I want to hear him say, *That's it, baby.*

I want to hear him say, *I love you, Rach.*

"Are you okay?" I ask him again.

He says nothing.

It is then I know it is over, for good.

Chapter Four: Coming Home

It's summer 2002. In a dire push to begin a new chapter of our lives, my little girl and I have moved back to my old stomping grounds in Northern California for a fresh start. I need to find a job. I need to find an apartment. I need to find a preschool for Mae.

I also need—make that want—to find a man. While this certainly isn't a necessity, it would be nice. I realize it would probably be best for Mae and me to be a team of two as we start our new life in the Bay Area, but I still hope we might find Mr. Right. It's never a good idea to hope someone will come along who will erase my ex from my memory—the classic definition of "on the rebound." All the same, it is mighty tempting.

I find a potential candidate at, of all places, the grocery store. He's a big African American guy working behind the fish counter. He wears a flannel shirt, rain boots, and plastic gloves. His baseball cap is backward. I spend two weeks and four outings checking him out.

Then one day, I push the cart past him, and our eyes meet. I smile, he smiles. Even Mae smiles.

A few months earlier, Mae and I had moved in with my dad in San Francisco while we got our bearings. This was my worst nightmare come true. Growing up, I'd always been an independent spirit, the all-honors kid in the suburbs who wore hiking boots under her shiny gold high school graduation gown. When I was eighteen, I dropped out of Reed College and moved to Mexico to teach English as a Second Language. Two years later, I got a job as a reporter for a newspaper in Connecticut. Then I moved to Prague in 1994 and wrote for the *Prague Post*.

I visited my parents once a year, if that, and rejected any financial support my father offered. I was proud of making it on my own. But now, as a single mother, I've needed to swallow my pride, at least temporarily.

When I got pregnant with Mae, I was a researcher at Time Inc.'s high-rise on 50th Street in Midtown Manhattan.

A few years later, I'm back under my father's roof, in *his* high-rise. Yes, I'm still attractive and smart—and single. But I live with my father. *And* my adorable toddler.

No man in his right mind will see me as a possible partner. C'mon, what kind of guy wants to date a single mom living with her dad, albeit temporarily? As they say in New York, *Forget about it.*

When we first land at my dad's, I spend every waking minute shouting to myself: *Why did you start things up with Eric again? Why did you let Victor go?* Breaking up with Victor was a terrible mistake, I fear. One month after our relationship officially ended in New York, he took off for New Mexico State University in Las Cruces to get a master's degree in statistics. He'd been planning to do this for a while, but kept the plan on hold for . . . well, for us. He is a good man, a good, goofy man. The last I heard from him was an email on Valentine's Day:

> *Rachel,*
> *I wish that we were together for just a couple of hours at least, so I could tell you all the ways that I am better from you and how rich you made me and how much I still love you and how much it hurts. . . . You are too damn hot to be alone for long and you'll find him and find it and find out. . . .*
> *Victor*

I printed out his words and taped them into my journal. I read them every day, holding on to his morsels of love. *Have I driven away the love of my life?* I wonder.

But we'd only dated for a few months. I'm not even sure why we broke up. Eric's return had freaked me out, and then Victor had regressed. I guess we'd both regressed.

I need to get over it.

Still, Victor's bonding with Mae felt priceless to me. I fear I've driven away a very good possibility of love.

After Victor left New York, I questioned why I was sticking around. Eric was still making empty promises to pay child support and be in Mae's life. And I was smarter now. Sure, I had an amazing group of friends. But they were leading their own busy lives. I needed more support. My family was out West.

When we move to California, I'm still up in the air, my head like a balloon inflating with constant thoughts: *Where will we live? How will I make money out here? Do I even know how to make friends all over again?*

I never stayed in touch with my childhood friends from the suburbs. I keep calling my girlfriends back in New York. They are far off, but my heart is still there; I want to do a U-turn and go back—though I know if I were there, I would want to be here. One of my friends tells me she ran into Eric—drunk—outside a bar. He is a lost cause. He's never given me a cent, either. So goodbye to Eric and all that. Mae and I need a fresh start.

My father has always been supportive of my decision to have Mae. He often said that he wished he could wave a magic wand and make everything right for us. Now he's one of her regular baby sitters. But it hasn't always been easy. We've never learned how to listen to each other without raising our voices.

When I went to college in 1990, my dad had a hard time letting me go. He called me every day, and sent me bouquets of flowers and tubs of flavored popcorn. Every time I said, "Stop," he said, "Go." While most people saw him as the most generous dad in the world, I felt smothered. Around that time, I started to sign my schoolwork as "Rachel Sarah"—my first name and middle name. No last name, no father. I liked it. Erasing my last name felt right in some mysterious way. I was no longer the girl who rode all day on Daddy's shoulders. I was unapologetically standing on my own two feet. I soon made my new name official: on my passport, my bank card, my driver's license, all my identification. Dropping his name was my way of saying, "I want my own life."

Now that I'm a grownup with a kid in tow, I don't know how to heal our relationship, but I want to. I realize I made some dramatic decisions in separating myself from him. But more and more, I want to clear the air and have him be a vital part of Mae's life. And since her birth, he's tried his best to be helpful and supportive. Dramatic, often, but also caring and loving.

One Sunday afternoon, the fog clears and I ask my dad if he wants to go on a walk around Pier 39 in San Francisco's Embarcadero. I push Mae in the stroller, as my dad and I talk about my dismal apartment search in the East Bay.

"I'm competing with all of these college students right now," I say. "It's hard."

Mae turns her head around. "No talking to Grandpa!" she says.

"I need to talk to him," I say.

"You're going about it all wrong. You're looking in the wrong neighborhood," my dad says.

"Why do you say that?" I ask defensively.

Mae turns around again: "No talking to Grandpa!"

"She's a control freak," my dad says.

"No, she's not!" I say.

"Yes, she is," he says. "Just listen to her. No other two-year-old talks like that."

"Her life has just been turned upside down," I say. "She's trying to get some order back."

"A little kid doesn't function like that," my dad says.

"How would you know?" I say, my voice getting louder.

"You're just justifying her behavior," Dad says, his voice getting louder.

And so it goes.

My dad has always been compulsive. He doesn't think before he speaks. Out of the blue, he'll tell me things like, "You're a terrible cook" or "You dress your daughter like a little beggar girl."

I hate riding around the city in the back of his fancy sports car. I hate asking him to buy Mae a new pair of shoes because the old ones pinch her toes. I hate watching him write out a check for a down payment on a car for me. I feel ashamed for being so privileged.

But I also realize how blessed I am; maybe I can get over the guilt. At least I can try. I also know that I am lucky to have his support. Other fathers might have shunned their daughters for having a baby out of wedlock. Or for choosing the wrong man. Not mine.

My first Mother's Day as a mother, my dad flew out to spend the weekend with us. He read books to one-year-old Mae and kissed her toes. As she piled sand from the playground sandbox on to her grandpa's black dress shoes, I wondered if I could ever really appreciate him.

Now Mae calls him "Pa." And she seems perfectly happy here, shacked up with her mom and grandpa, playing hide-and-seek, eating applesauce, and walking down to the pier to watch the sea lions.

Every day, I am in awe of Mae, who has just turned two and already is learning how to use the potty. She loves to peel back the stickers on her diaper and let it drop to the rug. She toddles around my dad's place naked. I chase after her little butt.

"Something's coming down the pike!" she says. She's off, around the corner, making her way to the plastic, light blue potty I lugged here from New York.

"You go, Mae!" I say, as I follow behind her into the bathroom.

Strangers always comment on her complex sentences and vocabulary. When she wants to nurse, she says, "Have some milk, please?" When I unfold the stroller to go outside, she wants to know, "Where we going, Mama?" When we enter a public place, she waves to strangers. She even greets the public restroom: "How you doing, potty? Nice to see you!"

One weekend, we drive with my dad up to Santa Rosa to visit Mae's older cousins, who give her a Barbie doll. She tears its clothes off and in a panicked voice asks, "Mama, where are her nipples?"

Nursing Mae is the only time I feel my body. I breastfeed "on demand," as they call it in the La Leche League books. There is no doubt my milk comforts her after a fall, makes her feel safe in the middle of the night, and tastes better than ice cream. She tells me so. But I know that I'm being nurtured, too. When my milk lets down, my toes buzz. It's the only time my thoughts slow down, milk flowing from me, proving that I can do this alone.

Being fatherless does not worry Mae. She isn't concerned about saying the "wrong" thing or loving people or making new friends. She is my fresh fruit, the constant bright spot in my day. She releases my pain. She makes me laugh.

Most of the time, my dad and Mae are like long-lost playmates. My dad has retired after selling his computer programming business, so he hangs out with us every day. He brings home presents for her: board books, plastic zoo animals, *Sesame Street* videos. Every night without fail, she dashes into his bedroom and pulls herself up on his bed.

"Pa!" she yells.

"Do I hear a monkey on my bed?" he asks in his deep monster voice.

"No!" she giggles.

"I hope there isn't a monkey on my bed!" he says.

"No!" she says. "Come and see!"

"I better not find a monkey on my bed!" he says.

She dives under his covers with a shriek. He pulls the blankets back. "I said, 'No monkeys on my bed!'" She screams, laughing. He hugs her. She melts into his arms.

"Again!" she says. "Again!"

Yes, I realize how lucky I am. As much as my dad can be a pain in the butt—and I still agonize over how to redefine our relationship—he's the best built-in baby sitter a mom could ask for.

And I have to confess: I realize that I've returned home because of him. Mae and I have come home to a man after all—it's just that it's my dad.

As much as Mae loves her live-in playmate—Grandpa—it is time for her to be with children her own age. It's absurd how competitive preschool admissions are out here—almost as bad as they are in New York.

As my dad chases Mae around his bed, I sit on his living room sofa and dial another preschool director.

"I'm sorry, we have no spots for the fall," she says. "Would you like to be added to the waiting list?"

I hang up the phone and stare out the window. I curl my arms around my ratty Levi's and know I can't give up. I've always envisioned myself as the kind of mother who would pick her daughter up at school and bring her home for a healthy snack. In the afternoon, we'd go out for a "color walk," picking up leaves and flowers to make a collage. After toddling around the neighborhood, we'd make a big pot of chicken noodle soup in our warm kitchen.

Even if life isn't working out the way I'd imagined, I have to keep trying. And I realize that as long as Mae and I have each other and—I have to admit it—my dad, we will be fine.

Thanks to our family friend Norine, Mae and I finally find a place of our own. I've known fiery, red-headed Norine since I was born—she and my father used to work together—and she was responsible for persuading me to move back to California, promising in her long letters to be Mae's "honorary grandma."

For weeks after we arrived in San Francisco, Norine drove us around to look at little, dark, dingy apartments, as I fed Mae crackers in the back seat. Now she has found us an apartment in North Berkeley, right across the street from her. It is a sunny, warm one-bedroom with a kitchen so big that Mae can learn to ride a tricycle in it.

Norine is a single mom who raised her son, who is my age. She tells me that single motherhood is perfect because you get to call all the shots. She says, "Sleep with men, but never marry one. They only get in your way." She says that Mae will turn out to be a brilliant and assertive girl because she gets my undivided attention. "There's no man around to compete with her."

Norine is one of the most assertive women I know, sometimes infuriatingly so, freely sharing her beliefs and opinions, even when I haven't asked.

Still, it is Norine who highly recommends the preschool at the Berkeley-Richmond Jewish Community Center because she's heard such amazing feedback from other neighborhood moms.

Although I've had nothing to do with Judaism for over a decade, I check out the preschool and am pleasantly surprised by its diversity: There are a few Eurasian kids, a Spanish-speaking girl, an African American boy. (Well, this *is* Berkeley, right?) The head teacher, a local painter and sculptor, gently puts her hand on my shoulder and says, "She'll do fine."

On her first day of preschool, Mae is wearing a pink T-shirt, turquoise OshKosh overalls, and shiny red boots. She's two-and-a-half years old. Her hair is wild and kinked out. I run to the bottom of the stairs with my camera. As she walks down the steps, I feverishly shoot photos of her.

"Cheese!" she says. The flash goes off again and again.

"Cheese!" she says. After a few minutes, she stops. "Enough pictures, Mommy."

At school, I give her a big kiss as we step inside the door. "See you soon!" I say.

"See you soon!" she says. She's not crying. She's not reaching for me. She turns around and toddles over to the book corner.

My heart is pounding, *Oh my baby, oh my little baby.* But I know she'll be just fine.

I walk over to Peet's Coffee & Tea on Vine Street and tell the young baristo, "My daughter started preschool today." He gives me a coffee on the house.

I'm freelancing for a couple of educational textbook publishers in New York. I also send out my résumé locally, responding to jobs through the National Writers Union. I land a gig with a therapist in San Jose, ghostwriting his book, *Conscious Dating: Finding the Love of Your Life in Today's World.* When he offers me the job on the phone, I think, *Me? Writing about dating? I've only been on a couple of dates in the past few years!* He also pays me to take his "Relationship Success Training for Singles" course to get a better understanding of his overall mission. Little do I know what this professional job will do for my personal life.

In the relationship classes, I have the chance to ponder, *Who am I? What do I want? How do I get what I want?*

At this point, it seems so simple. I just want to sleep with a man. He'll make me come alive. He'll give me a break from my mommy role for a while. He'll bring me back into my body. A mighty tall order, I realize.

But maybe I'm not thinking straight. After all, I haven't slept with a man since Victor, boyfriend No. 1. I'm going on Day 182.

Since Mae and I arrived in California, we've been happy to be among friends and family. My dad isn't the only support I have here in the Bay Area. My sister, Rebecca, who's just seventeen months younger than I am, lives in San Francisco, too. Our relationship has gone through many jealous, intense phases, but we're in a good place now. She's certainly a doting aunt.

These first few months, I've dedicated myself to creating a home for us, reconnecting with my dad, spending more time outside, and getting freelance work. It's also been a total culture shock from New York—and that includes the kind of men I've been meeting. Most of them are guys I see every day and don't give much thought to—the man at the hardware store or the video store, the mailman.

I'm not really looking to hook up the day I meet Tom, who works behind the fish counter at the Berkeley Bowl, our local grocery store. Boy, am I out of practice with meeting men.

One Friday afternoon, I muster the courage to walk up to him and say a real "hello." If I'd had my wits about me, I would have paused for a second to see what he was selling. I have to stand on my tiptoes to talk. "One chicken breast, please," I say.

"I'm sorry, but we don't sell breasts *here*," he says, laughing.

My cheeks go red. I look down at the counter and see oysters, salmon, and crabs. But no chicken.

He points over to the poultry counter. "You'll have to go over there."

"Oh, I'm sorry, I . . . "

My fingers go limp around the shopping cart. Jeesh, what's wrong with me? I can't do something as simple as flirt with the fish man.

"Excuse me, ma'am, are you done?" a customer says behind me.

I don't hear anyone. Mae is still humming, but I don't hear her, either. There's just a blur of fish eyes, shiny scales, and blocks of ice. I vaguely notice the customer behind me has moved on to another counter. *Why can't I move?*

"Now that we got that out of the way," the cute fish man is saying, "I'd love to get your number."

"My number?" I turn around to make sure he's not talking to someone behind me.

I write it down on a piece of paper and pass it over the counter.

Well, what do you know? Maybe that accidental ice breaker worked?

After a phone conversation, he suggests we get together some-time. "Why not sushi?" I suggest in keeping with the fish theme.

So here I am the following Friday night at 6:30, racing through an irritatingly sluggish Berkeley rush hour. I've traded my sweatpants and T-shirt ensemble for a snug, knee-length jean skirt and cotton tank top. I even found a matching pair of silver earrings in the bottom of a moving box. I can't remember the last time I wore long earrings like these. They feel so strange that I keep reaching up to touch my earlobes, certain that my daughter has stuck Play-Doh to my ears. I've left my dad and Mae at home on the sofa, watching *Mary Poppins.*

It's a balmy fall night, and this is officially my first date since moving to California. I get to the restaurant at seven on the dot and wait outside. I wait five minutes. And then ten minutes.

I stare at my watch, as I lean back against the wall. Normally, I'd be cuddled up in bed with my little girl about now, nursing her to sleep. I'd be drifting off myself, after a full day of getting Mae dressed, packing her preschool lunch, walking her down the hill to school, getting back for a day of textbook editing, picking her up, battling to get her to take a nap, and then giving up, pushing the stroller to the playground for an hour on the swings, then returning for a dinner of noodles and "sprinkle-sprinkle" cheese.

Where is this guy? I'm tired of waiting. Doesn't he realize how precious my time is? I know I'm being impatient and tell myself to mellow out. Pre-baby, my schedule wasn't so dear to me; I had the whole night ahead of me. A date could turn into a couple of drinks, maybe an all-nighter. When Tom jogs up fifteen minutes later in blue jeans and a ratty T-shirt, I'm deflated. Still, I love his sparkling brown eyes and brawny arms.

He leans over to kiss my cheek. It's so unexpected that I bend to the side, swiping his ear.

"I'm sorry," I say, startled.

Without the counter between us, there's no shield. The counter was my permanent bodyguard. It let us flirt without physical contact. Now it's gone, and I'm not sure quite how to navigate these new waters.

"No, *I'm* so sorry," he says. "My car's having transmission problems."

"What's wrong with it?"

"It only goes forward, but not in reverse. I had to circle around to find a parking space."

I stifle a laugh, but I have to wonder about this: the fact that he's only moving forward. Is this good on some metaphysical level?

Inside, we're seated at a two-person table in the back, where we both stare hard at our menus. I'm even afraid to look up, not knowing what to say that doesn't have to do in some way with fish. I realize that I know nothing about him, except that he works behind the fish counter.

"I don't eat raw fish," he says suddenly. "I can't stomach it after working with the dead stuff all day."

"Okay," I say, wondering why we're eating here. Why didn't he say something earlier? We steer clear of fish and instead order chicken teriyaki and *udon* soup.

I find out that he loves video games and topographic maps, both of which he collects. He likes to drink dark beer and sleep until noon on his days off. He tells me about his asshole manager at Berkeley Bowl and his unpaid parking tickets.

So far, I'm not detecting any overlapping interests. I haven't played a video game since high school, have a hard time reading maps, don't really like dark beer, and consider sleeping until 7:30 AM a luxury. He doesn't ask me any questions, either about being a single mom or anything else. Not an auspicious start.

I want to tell Tom that I love being a mom, even when it's really hard. I want to tell him about the finger painting Mae did today. I want to tell him what her teacher said when I arrived for pickup: "Mae is such a thoughtful little girl. She came up to me today and said, 'What's God?'"

But I bite my tongue. As my friend Siobhan will eventually say, if I start planning my wedding with him right now, it would be like going to the hardware store for milk. Here's a man sitting across from me, but that doesn't mean he's the one to tell all my deepest fears or all Mae's triumphs.

An hour into our date, I know that Tom will never come to my home or meet my daughter. Our relationship will be emotionally uncomplicated. Yes, this will be simple. The act of sex is always simple for me. It's what comes afterward that's hard. When I'm in a relationship with a man, I have expectations. Relationships for me are not straightforward.

After our un-amazing dinner and run-of-the-mill conversation, we walk out to the lot where both our cars are parked. I just want to get home to Mae and my dad. Maybe I can even catch the last part of *Mary Poppins.*

"I want to show you this amazing map I got in the mail today," he says, interrupting my thoughts.

"Sure," I say, without thinking. I follow him to his hatchback, knowing that he probably wants to show me more than just his map. And I guess I'm curious. He is a cute guy, and it's been almost a year since I've had sex.

"It's a copy of a thousand-year-old topographic map from Asia," he says, as I climb into his back seat. I haven't been in a back seat with a guy since I was fifteen. I've definitely come down in the world.

Our thighs touch as he pulls the map open on our knees. It's so dark that we can't see it at all. I want to tell him, "Way to go." It's actually pretty ingenious how he got me in here for a make-out session.

"Cool," I say. I have to say that I like his quirky side.

He folds the map back up and puts his arm around me. Our faces meet under the faint glow of the street light.

I like the way his hand grips my thigh. I like the way he nibbles my bottom lip when he kisses me.

I even make it home for the end of *Mary Poppins*. As I hold Mae on my lap, I daydream. A little physical closeness hit the spot tonight, even if this guy isn't boyfriend material.

A week later, Tom invites me over for brunch on his day off. I drop Mae off at preschool, then head for Tom's. I have two hours to spare before I need to get home and email a freelance project to my editor in New York. As I drive to Tom's, I remind myself that this is going to be fun, safe, and uncomplicated. I'm horny, I have condoms, and I have some free time—I'm ready. In the last week, we've had a few phone conversations where I've learned a bit more about him: He can cook, and he finds me sexy. Bonus points for him. When I confess that I never bought a chicken from Berkeley Bowl because I never learned how to prepare a whole bird, he says, "I'm going to teach you how to make a chicken." (He never does, which is a shame, but at the time I'm touched by the offer.)

"You're so sexy," he has told me more than once.

As I walk into his apartment on Hearst Street, I'm ready to leave motherhood behind. I'm ready to abscond from nursing, mashing sweet potatoes, and singing *Sesame Street* tunes.

I expect to find him over a hot stove, flipping eggs. But there's just a pile of dishes in the sink.

"I'm sorry," he says. "I forgot about making you breakfast."

"That's okay," I say, even though my belly is growling. I try not to be irritated and to remember what I'm here for. But it's difficult.

His dirty clothes are in a heap under the window, and his clean clothes are in another heap on the sofa. There's a box of condoms next to an ashtray on the floor. Can you say b-a-c-h-e-l-o-r? I'm tempted to do some straightening up, but decide to get to the task at hand. After all, I have only a limited amount of time.

When we stretch out side by side, I smell his sticky hair gel, a mix of coconut and wax. He wraps his big hands around my waist.

"You make my pants move," he says.

I giggle. "No man has ever said it like that before!"

He pulls my jeans off and reaches between my thighs and touches me gently for a while. I climb on top of him and straddle his sides. I close my eyes and try to let go. Luckily, I'm blessed with the ability to get aroused easily, especially when I don't have a regular sex life.

I'm eager to be here, where I can be off duty from motherhood for this moment. His mouth tastes like a thin-skinned apple. I'm hot and wet. This is going to be swift and fast. He traces his fingers over my nipple and licks the tip. I rock back and forth on his hips, as he swells up inside of me. I ask him to hold my ass. He does. My belly tingles and I swing myself hard into him. It doesn't take me long to build up a rhythm. With his hands all over me, I reach the brink quickly.

When I walk back to my car, my cheeks are glowing, and I feel ready and rejuvenated for an afternoon of editing.

It's not that I love Tom—nowhere close in fact. I just love the fact that he knows the woman in me—and not the mom. When I'm with Tom, it's my short-lived exit from motherhood. When he kisses my nipples, he doesn't know that for more than two years, they have been a milk store, open 24/7. He just knows that they're sensitive and for his—and my—enjoyment. He doesn't know how my expression changes when my daughter falls or bumps her head, or how I cradle her in my arms and kiss her boo-boos. He doesn't know how my limbs soften when I hear her say the word, "Mama." But the point of our affair is that he's not supposed to know.

He appreciates my body and my mind, with an emphasis on body. And I feel the same. I love licking his muscular chest. I love gripping his ropy-veined arms. I love taking his fingers between my lips like candy canes. I love pushing my nipple into his mouth. *Whew* . . . it's getting *hot* in here.

Over the next couple of months, I love calling on Tom for a quickie when he has a day off. This fits both our needs. And though the romantic in me is still open to finding that perfect match, for now the pragmatic part of me is okay with this arrangement. Being with Tom satisfies me the way an energy bar does. I know I should eat a healthier, more balanced meal, but for now this will do.

On a Friday afternoon, exactly two months after our first date, Tom and I walk down to College Avenue for a slice of pizza after some particularly wild sex.

"I'm weaning Mae," I tell him.

"Weaning?" he says.

"I'm not going to be nursing her anymore," I explain. "It's been almost three years now."

"Oh," he says.

I know that he doesn't get it, but against my better judgment, I keep trying. "My hormones are crazy right now," I tell him.

It's true. I've never experienced anything like this before. I've never been the kind of mom who raises her voice, but suddenly I am.

"Don't!" I say when Mae unties her shoelaces right after I've tied them. "Stop!" I say as she pulls clean laundry from the dryer and tosses it onto the kitchen floor.

"Something's out of whack inside me," I tell Tom. I want to tell him how guilty I feel for losing it with Mae. How my nerves are off kilter and my patience is short. One moment, I'm bawling because my nipples are tender. The next moment, my uterus feels like it will catch fire if I don't have sex with him soon.

"Oh," he says, looking bewildered. He doesn't get it.

Fortunately, I've met two moms in Berkeley who *do* get what I'm talking about.

A few days before my thirtieth birthday, I spot Siobhan at Totland, a North Berkeley playground. It isn't easy to miss her, in her red, fleece, flying cape, strolling her daughter, wearing a similar cape, complete with polka dots, and a matching fleece hat.

We quickly exchange stats and find out that her daughter, Hazel, is just a month younger than Mae. They also share the same middle name, Frances.

Siobhan pulls out the most amazing snack bag—a mix of dried fruits and crackers—which she offers to share with us *after* we clean our hands with the "wipies" she supplies. I wish I could pull out healthier snack options from my bag. I'm embarrassed to say that my snacks often consist of Quaker Chewy Chocolate Chip Granola Bars or sugar-loaded yogurt.

"Hey, Siobhan!" one mother says.

"How are you, Siobhan?" another mother says.

I soon learn that Siobhan, the owner of a kids' clothing store on Telegraph Avenue, is well known around town. She's the epitome of funky. She makes her own clothes, as well as many of her daughter's. Most of her designs are fleece, and they often include a piece of vibrant fake fur. As someone who never learned how to sew, I'm in awe of her. (When I invite her to my birthday party a few days later, she sews me a shoulder bag with a blue sky and puffy white clouds on it.)

We become fast friends, as do our girls. We have much in common—our daughters, our similar codependent relationships with men, and our love lives. I tell her about trying to get over my ex and landing here just a few months ago from New York City. She tells me about maneuvering through her painful divorce and filling out the messy legal work.

"I'm also weaning my daughter," she says.

"Me, too!" I say.

We trade tactics bribing our daughters with anything but breast milk: warm milk with vanilla, chocolate milk, ice cream. We talk about sleep deprivation, and the fact that it's used on war prisoners.

Siobhan also has a good bullshit detector and will in the coming years serve as a barometer for my bad taste in men. She'll say, "I was so drawn to you when we first met! But your taste in men was awful!" I can always count on her for her straight, up-front manner.

If Siobhan is my conscience when it comes to affairs of the heart, then Arden is my partner in crime.

I meet Arden and her daughter at UC Berkeley's Strawberry Canyon Pool. Like Siobhan, Arden stands out. But this is because she and her daughter look like a match to Mae and me. Arden is a white, single mom, like me, with brown hair and green eyes.

Her daughter, Celia, who is two when we meet, is biracial, like Mae, with coffee-brown skin and curly hair.

Arden sends me emails that say things like, "I'm so lucky that my girl has you all as part of her family."

Like Siobhan, Arden is well known around town because she manages the Sports4Kids Swap Shop, a nonprofit youth sports organization.

Both Arden and Siobhan are three years older than I am. They both like to tease me about being *so* young.

Thanks to my new friends, I'm immediately connected to a network of moms around the East Bay. More than that, I'm grateful for being part of this self-made single-moms' group. This isn't Gymboree or a baby-sitting co-op. Sure, we swap kids if one of us has to run an errand. But it's more than that. We call or email each other almost every day. Every Tuesday night, we get together for dinner and talk. One of us makes the main dish, while the others bring the sides and drinks. We take turns filling each other in about maternal woes, work stress, and latest dates.

I tell Siobhan and Arden about Mae's tantrums as I try to wean her.

I tell them how she pulls at my breasts, screaming, "I want my milk!"

"Let me rub your back, honey," I say.

"No! I want my milk!"

"Let me sing you a song," I say.

"No!" she screams.

"Quiet!" I say, raising my voice. "You're waking up the whole neighborhood!"

Mae doesn't know how to fall asleep without nursing. *What have I done?* She can't sleep unless my boob is in her mouth. But my nipples are red and sore. My breasts are stretched out and depleted. She sucks and sucks, but there's hardly any milk left.

I rub her back. I kiss her forehead. I draw mermaids between her shoulder blades. I talk about her day. I start driving her around at night, trying to get her to sleep. But I'm having a hard time letting go, too. I've gotten used to the oxytocin, how attached I feel, the way my body heats up as my milk lets down. I don't know how to let go of nursing, either.

After another afternoon quickie with Tom, he walks me to my car. My thighs are pounding from our workout. I feel spent, energized, ready to go. I lean into him for a kiss. But he jumps back.

I miss. I'm laughing. But he looks angry.

"Don't do that," he says.

"Don't do what?" I say.

"Kiss me first," he says. "I like to be the first."

"You're kidding," I say.

"No."

"I don't get it," I say. "Why didn't you tell me this before?"

"You never tried it before."

I cross my arms across my chest.

"Don't take it personally," he says.

But I do. The tears well up in my eyes.

"Don't be a crybaby," he says.

This pisses me off. The combination of my raging hormones and exhaustion brings the relationship to an end. I call it off, just like that. I stop returning his phone calls. I never go back to his place. A quickie once or twice a week isn't worth it. Though I don't rule out glorified hookups forever, I realize how unfulfilling they are. I want chocolate mousse, not a Hershey bar.

I decide that maybe my man is waiting for me online.

In late 2002, this is still a relatively new way to meet a guy. On Valentine's Day 2000, *Time* magazine reported, "Valentines may now be wired, but online dating is also fostering some very 19th century courtship." Something about online dating seems so safe to me, with the computer serving as a chaperon, "plenty of conversation but no touching," like "19th century parlors where couples sit in chairs and chat."

With my writing experience, maybe online dating will give me an edge? In 2001, *Newsweek* published a feature titled, "Love Online: Millions are turning to the Internet to find romance":

Online dating is more convenient and comfortable than scouring dreary Manhattan bars and haranguing friends to set up.

Amen.

Large sites like Matchmaker.com, AmericanSingles.com, and Match.com are exploding. Maybe it's time for me to hop on board? Online dating could be my "new frontier," and I'm always up for a new adventure. I feel psyched. A little.

On a cold Tuesday night in late December, our single-moms' potluck dinner is at my place. We've just finished eating spaghetti and tofu meatless sauce, so very Berkeley. The girls are playing with dolls in the other room, out of earshot.

"Online?" Siobhan says. "Why would you do that?"

"I want to get myself out there," I say.

Arden smiles. "If you do it, I'll do it."

I'm always up for a good dare. That's all it takes for me to go for it.

We have our photo shoot the following Tuesday at Arden's house. Siobhan wants *no* part in this online dating gig.

"I have to smell a man!" she tells us. "You can't do that on a computer screen!"

But she does offer to be our photographer.

I borrow some lipstick from Arden and try to look natural in her armchair, wearing a blue sweatshirt and jeans. Our three girls strip out of their clothes and play tag naked. Mae wants to brush my hair and put it in pigtails. Celia insists on putting lipstick on Arden, smearing it all over her upper lip.

Siobhan buzzes around Arden's bedroom, snapping photos on a digital camera. I'm smiling, ready for the camera, but my nude daughter squirms on my knees.

"Take my picture!" Mae says. "Take my picture!"

"Smile!" Arden tells me. "You look beautiful!"

But I need a haircut. I need a nap.

"It's too dark," Siobhan says. I move into the sofa chair near the window. But just when the light is right, bare Mae jumps into my lap again.

At the end of the night, only a couple of photos turn out well.

Still, this will be my New Year's resolution: to date.

Chapter Five:
Single Mom Seeking

"Warm, generous single mom seeking respectful, cooperative man with both feet on the ground who dreams big." This is how my profile begins.

Within three days, I have my first Match.com date.

I pull off my work-at-home uniform—a pair of worn Levi's and a tank top—and trade it for a bright crimson slit skirt and matching top. No, that doesn't look right; it's *way* too sexy for a first date. How about a pair of Levi's in better condition? That might be more like it.

As I lean into the closet, Mae is coming at me with a ponytail scrunchie, a holdover from the eighties.

"Honey, you're hurting me!" I say as she pulls on my hair.

"This is *so* pretty, Mommy," she says of the rainbow scrunchie.

"Enough," I say. I haven't even gotten dressed for my date yet, and I'm already exasperated.

"I need to find something to wear!" I say.

Mae doesn't know what a date is. "Mommy is going out for coffee," I tell her. Since it's not hot chocolate, she's not disappointed. What are you supposed to tell your three-year-old when you're going out on a date? I've been reading the single-parent dating guides out there; none seems to apply to single moms with very young children.

Here's a sampling of the advice that Siobhan, Arden, and I can find irrelevant to our situation:

Don't share inappropriately with your children. (Duh!)

Have regular family discussions with your children. (Excuse me?)

Do not use them as "confidantes" for your relationship confusion or problems. (As if I'd come home and cry on her little shoulder . . .)

At least I was smart enough to ask Siobhan and Arden for feedback on my Match.com profile before I posted it. Besides, they would have killed me if I hadn't.

I am a 31-year-old single mom who loves picnics in the sunshine, staying up late with a good book, and sitting in the steam room. . . .

Arden writes back, "Love it!" Siobhan, however, immediately vetoes the "steam room."

"It smacks of sex," she says.

"C'mon!" I say. "I meant after a good workout," which I realize makes it sound worse. Two double entendres in a row. Still, I trust Siobhan—and nix the steam room.

The first rule of placing an ad I learn is not to leave anything open to interpretation. Be clear and straightforward. But Siobhan does let me get away with saying that I also love "anything curried, *café con leche,* and long embraces."

She's also okay with my telling online strangers that I'm "bilingual in Spanish, petite, and healthy in mind and body."

But when I check off that one of my turn-ons is "skinny-dipping," she shakes her head.

"Skinny-dipping is a big *no-no*," she says.

"Why?"

"It implies one thing and one thing only," she says. "Sex."

"I love skinny-dipping!" I protest.

Siobhan shoots me one of her mother-looks, usually reserved for her daughter. Still, I'm doubtful: Won't I come across as conservative and uninteresting if I just say, "Hi. I'm a mom. Want to go out on a date?"

I also will learn eventually that the direct route is the way to go.

But for now, I go for the gusto when I write about the kind of man I'm looking for:

I am hopeful for a deep and honest friendship that could bloom into a relationship. You are any race. You don't use drugs. You are an open and honest man who loves to cook and eat homemade meals, go on adventures to new places, walk in the woods, and give warm hugs. You are responsible, cooperative, and affectionate.

You adore children. I imagine being each other's cheerleaders.

Siobhan applauds. Then we clink our wineglasses together and drink to love.

One of the first email messages to arrive in my in-box from Match.com seems promising.

Just read your profile and wanted to tell you that I have been looking for someone like you. Something about the strength of a single mother is very attractive to me. Please read my profile and drop me a note if the spirit moves you.

I feel rewarded, but also nervous. This stranger has no idea that at the end of every day, I am run ragged—bags under my eyes, unwashed hair, and spaghetti sauce spotting my blouse. As I glance around our tiny apartment from my desk, I can see yesterday's sandwich crusts still on the kitchen counter and stray crayons under the table.

Just last night, Mae was screaming, "But I don't want to go to bed like a big girl!"

"Then you can go to nap room tomorrow like a baby!" I screamed back, immediately feeling like a horrible mom.

Then I notice the P.S. at the bottom of the email: "My profile says I prefer women a bit older than you . . . but there are exceptions to everything."

I can see my smile reflected in my computer screen. Don't we all love the thrill of being someone's exception?

I devour his profile: "I'm 40. Happiness is not terribly complicated for me. A warm place. Coffee in the morning with something to read. The observations of someone I find wise." He is a divorced businessman who likes bluegrass music, movies that make him sad, old things, sunshine on his face, and being warm.

His name is Gary, and in our first few emails, we discover that we both played the saxophone in high school and often hike through Tilden Park. I notice how often he use ellipses . . . I do that, too!

Gary wants to get together for a glass of wine, but I am cautious. I don't drink very much, and just one glass of wine tilts me off balance. I will have to leave my car at home and take a taxi. Certainly, he will insist on driving me home, and I picture him turning off the motor and kissing me.

In the past, the thought of meeting a man I didn't know across town in a small, dark bar pumped me up. I would have jumped on a wild night like this. But I am turning thirty-one this year. I want more than just quick sex with the fish man. I am ready to be friends first. I am ready to talk about my kid.

I am ready to introduce him to my best friends. I am ready to cook a spicy stir-fry together and share a glass of wine. I am ready to make him worth my time. My bottom line: He and I have to have more in common than a carnal connection. Yes, I want something more.

I suggest a phone conversation with Gary first. After I am sure Mae is asleep, I call him on my cell phone. Our voices ricochet as if in an echo chamber. At first I can't hear what he is saying.

"What? Can you repeat that?" My voice is tight, constricted with nerves.

"I said, 'Am I your first Match boy?'"

I laugh. "Is it that obvious?"

In the photos, Gary looks nothing like the men I'm usually attracted to. Eric is a six-foot-tall African American construction worker. Gary is a five-foot-six white guy with graying temples. From our conversations I know he is a Virginia native with a strong Southern accent. After a comfortable round of emails, I finally agree to meet him in person.

That night, I can't get to sleep. I stare at the streetlight outside my window. My legs are jittery, and I kick the sheets off. I am way too hot. I can't stop thinking about Gary. I am still in the early throes of the wonder of Match.com, confident that I'll find a man there. I'm probably overly enthusiastic, thinking I can simply order a man as if he were the tastiest entrée on the menu.

At midnight, I get up and turn on my computer. There is another email from Gary: "I keep thinking about tomorrow like it's Christmas morning, and I'm ten," he writes. "Only with more trepidation."

I hold my breath. Now, I'll really never get to sleep.

The next morning, I arrive at Café Roma five minutes early. I choose this meeting place because it allows me to stay in line with the online-safety dating rules I've been studying: "Pick a public place and provide your own transportation."

I also tell Siobhan where I'm going and promise to check in with her when I get home.

"I'm going to drive by and spy on you," she says.

"Please don't!" I beg.

"But I love you," she says. "What if he's a psycho killer?"

"I'm sure he's fine," I say.

"You can never be sure."

This whole process feels so time-consuming and exhausting already—and I haven't even met the guy.

I scan the café, searching for that man who matches the online photo. Is that him, with the gray blazer? No, I don't think so. How about that guy, with the steaming mug of coffee? After such a restless night, I can't see straight.

I inhale when I see him walk around the corner. He looks just like my father did fifteen years ago. It's uncanny; they are exactly the same height, with thick salt-and-pepper hair. At first, I want to rush the other way, stand him up, just get out of here. Dating a man who reminds me so much of my father? Not. But then I remember how much we seem to have in common and my desire to date someone more stable and dependable than the slackers I've been with.

Gary walks right past me sitting on a bench outside the busy café. I stand and follow him. When he recognizes me, he hugs me in the doorway of the café while customers squeeze past. Then we sit down and both decide on oatmeal with maple syrup. Midway into breakfast, he tells me that he had a tumor in his one of his lungs last year. He's been through surgery and chemo, and he is cancer-free now.

"Are you okay?" I ask. I want to reach out and give him a hug. But I am wondering if he's too old for me.

"I went through a really rough patch there," he says. "I still take all kinds of medications, but I'm running again for the first time in eighteen months."

Yikes. Can I handle a man with cancer along with the rest of my life?

He tells me that he is going to be forty-one on Monday. It's not like I haven't dated men who were much older than I. Mae's father is thirteen years older. I don't place too much meaning on numbers. I'm looking for a stable and dependable man right now. Does this come with age? Sometimes. And sometimes not. I laugh. "So, then you'll be a whole decade older than me!"

"Please don't say that."

Then I remind myself this is only our first date. My entire dating life, I have conveniently skipped the dating part of relationships. After the initial oh-this-is-fun-and-he-adores-me, I have fallen deeply in love, ready to commit my life to someone. But not anymore. Well, at least some of the time.

Maybe motherhood is changing me. It's not just about *me* anymore. My daughter is a part of me. I can't just put her on the shelf when I go on a date. What will she think of a new man in our lives? Will she like him? Or see him as an intrusion? And will he respect her? Will this man understand that, for me, *her* needs will always come before his?

Maybe Gary is right. There is something about the strength of a single mother.

I go on two more dates with Gary. I love writing emails to him late at night, but I don't feel any goose bumps.

"I wish you were in my weekend," he says. But Mae has a fever that Saturday, and I need to stay home with her.

"I'm very glad I found you," he writes.

Why don't I feel the same way?

During our next Tuesday Girls Night Out, I tell Siobhan and Arden that there's no chemistry.

"You can't fake it," Siobhan says.

"What if you try a first kiss just to see how it feels?" Arden says.

I make a yucky face. I just don't see it happening.

I take him out for dinner on his forty-first birthday and down a whole glass of wine. This is a wild move for a lightweight like me. Still, my heart just isn't pounding. I've never understood why I'm attracted to certain people over others. Does he have to make me laugh? Or, as Siobhan says, is it really how he smells? Maybe it is all about pheromones. I can't seem to help whom I'm attracted to, even if we're wildly incompatible.

I know this about Gary: I can't imagine leaning up against a light post and kissing him passionately. Or sailing with him across the Pacific Ocean. Or simply bringing him home.

Maybe he resembles my father too much. Maybe he talks too much about business. There's a little peck on the lips, but never a real kiss. No fire to put out.

But I am not about to give up that easily.

After putting Mae to sleep every night, I stay up and read the notes that arrive from at least a handful of new men every day on Match.com. My fingers work at high speed as I sit at my computer way past my bedtime. This is more than fascinating. I feel like I'm on a treasure hunt. I love the anonymity of it all, as I stretch out in my panties and T-shirt, the minutes ticking by, my fingers tapping out responses. The reader in me loves examining all these details about men before meeting them. The writer in me loves drafting witty notes. It feels so safe to be checking men out from my living room. I scroll through hundreds of them, clicking on their photos.

This is my new drug, my remedy for late-night loneliness. I'm addicted to all the attention.

For some reason, I mostly hear from never-married guys who live in the suburbs. They tell me about grilling hamburgers on their barbeques and playing golf. They remind me of my church-going stepfather: Their favorite author is Dean Koontz, they love red meat, and they drive SUVs. I just don't see the match. They tend to be in their late thirties or early forties. (The very first line of my profile states that I'm a single mom; maybe this has weeded out guys my own age.) But, hey, at least they're not the bad boys I usually go for.

I can't stomach typos. I say "no thank you" to men who write, "i'm very frendly . . . I dont drink . . ." I delete the men who send me notes that were obviously predrafted and mailed out en masse: "I do fell [sic] that I may be the one for you. Maybe the one you have been seeking. Please check my profile. You may be interested." Total turn-off.

Forget about the men whose profiles say they'd go out with women as young as eighteen. *Yuck.*

Little things, too, are automatic turn-offs. Like men who post photos of themselves with their arms around another woman. Or the men who don't even bother writing anything in their profiles—they just make mandatory check marks indicating they want a twenty-one- to thirty-two-year old, fit woman.

So, this is what dating is all about: looking for red flags, obeying red flags, running like hell when I see one, asking questions, talking about myself without revealing too much. It makes me feel alternately exhilarated and exhausted.

Thirty-nine-year-old Benjamin from Richmond says that he "will not play games" and is "straightforward about things." He sure is. When I write back, he asks straight off if we can meet tonight. Hold on there, buddy! We haven't even talked on the phone yet.

A fisherman in Benicia says that he doesn't drink or use drugs. But he is wearing a nicotine patch right now to quit smoking, he adds. He invites me on his boat this Sunday. No thanks.

Forty-year-old Jaipal is an accountant who lives in Walnut Creek, the suburb where I grew up. He also plays golf. But where's the spunk?

As my mom always says, "Any man who goes out with you *has* to have personality!"

Amen to that.

Chapter Six:
Red-Flag Alert

One month into Match.com, my sister, Rebecca, is on her way here from San Francisco to baby-sit. It's Valentine's Day. How exciting to have a blind date on Valentine's Day.

"Is this another Match boy?" she wants to know.

A guy named Robby "winked" at me after seeing my photo and profile, and sent me an instant message. At first I thought this was charming, but started to find it annoying. As soon as I saw Robby's photo, however, I forgot all about how much I disliked getting winked at. He looks like a Calvin Klein ad. He has a boyish smile, dirty blond hair, and straight, white teeth.

Robby's profile says, "I'm sober and working on being unselfish, an ideal toward which I constantly strive and hope you might appreciate."

Robby, forty-two, is a waiter who lives in the Mission. He goes to AA meetings twice a week. He seems like the perfect match for me, a woman who includes in her own headline, "Are you addiction-free?"

He writes, "I'm open to who God puts in my path as long as she doesn't need citizenship and speaks English."

We email back and forth, and I think he's witty. We talk on the phone one evening and realize that both of us are date-less for Valentine's Day. How perfect. It's a match.

But when my sister arrives, and I let her take a peek, she isn't laughing.

"Look at how sincere he is," I say. I point to the part where Robby writes, "I am here to be with one extremely focused communicative woman who wants to hang in there and reveal herself, not censor her thoughts and act strategically."

Yes, that's the kind of woman I want to be. My ideal relationship is one in which we are present for each other; we sit and talk; we are vulnerable and open.

But my sister is shaking her head. "He's just trying to feed somebody a line," she says.

I point out to her how hilarious he is. Under "favorite hot spots," he writes, "the sauna, the stove, the oven, the hot-water heater, the sun, the equator, the tropics, Madagascar, LA's tar pits . . ."

I, on the other hand, have replied to the same category, "My local hot spot is the playground."

But my sister isn't even smiling.

"It's just a first date," I tell her.

"Be careful," she says. "It's not just about you anymore, you know."

"I know," I say. "I'm the big sister around here, in case you forgot."

"Keep your head on your shoulders tonight, okay?"

I'm defensive. All those nervous jitters are gone. I turn on the shower. Just as I'm stepping out, my cell phone rings.

It's Robby. "What are you wearing?" he asks.

"Excuse me?" Is this a come-on? "I'm not sure. Does it matter?"

"Because I'm getting all dressed up," he says. "I'm wearing the suit that I wore to my friend's wedding last summer." The suit that he wore to a wedding? What does that mean? Does he expect me to get dressed up in wedding attire, too? A flowery strapless dress? A silky gown? Heels and nylons? We're going to see a movie downtown. I look at the outfit I've hung from the towel rack in the bathroom: a tight corduroy skirt, a pink, knit sweater with a low V-neck, and black boots. If you ask me, it looks like the perfect first-date outfit. It's cute and feminine, with a touch of sexiness. Who is this guy? I haven't even met him, and he's pressuring me to get all dolled up.

I put on my planned outfit anyhow. In the kitchen, my sister is spooning out another serving of mac and cheese for Mae.

"Mommy, you're so pretty!" Mae says.

Ah, that girl is good. I give her a big peck on the cheek and race down the stairs. In the car, I try to remember the reasons I agreed to go out with him in the first place. I want to turn around and go back home, but I've got to psyche myself up. Robby is a movie buff. He told me about his plan to make a documentary film about the high rate of breast cancer in Marin. I'm impressed.

I suggested we see a movie tonight. *The Dreamers* is playing downtown. I get to the theater at 6:30 and wait outside. The minutes pass. The more dates I go on, the more I realize that being late is a bad sign. A man who's behind schedule will never really be there for you. Unless he's caught in some dire emergency, there's no excuse. I go up to the window and buy tickets for both of us.

Fifteen minutes later, my phone rings.

"Hi, I'm looking for parking," Robby says.

Here he comes, in his shiny taupe suit and white, big-collared shirt with the top two buttons undone. His black dress shoes glimmer in the dark. Sticking out in the Mission, for sure! "Hi, Rachel," he says, handing me a red rose. "Happy Valentine's Day."

He opens his arms to give me a hug.

"Thanks," I say, falling halfway into his long arms. It's always awkward knowing how to greet a man on a blind date. But on

Valentine's Day it's especially awkward. He holds on to me for ten long seconds, his six-foot frame leaning over me. My nose is buried in his smooth jacket.

When we let go, I look up at him. "You are cute," I say. But I think to myself, *Damn, he looks at least a decade older than in his photo.* There are crow's feet around his eyes, and his skin is rough from the sun. His hairline is receding.

We go inside, and he buys the popcorn. Little do I know how inappropriate *The Dreamers* is for a first date. A nineteen-year-old American moves to Paris in the late 1960s and dives into a relationship with a pair of amoral and incestuous twins. Our fingers dig into the popcorn as the characters make passionate love.

I know that certainly won't be Robby and me.

The red rose that Robby gave me on Valentine's Day sits next to the mattress on the floor where Mae and I sleep. When I brought it home, Mae said, "Thank you, Mommy!" Its buds are starting to open.

The day after our date, Robby calls and tells me he'd like to see me again. I accept, though I have to admit that he doesn't get me all hot and bothered—at least not yet. I'm drawn to his Calvin Klein smile and deep voice. And I like the fact that he doesn't drink. After being with Eric, this seems like a healthy choice. He's committed to AA; maybe this means he can commit to a woman, too?

On Sunday, I drop Mae off at Arden's house before meeting Robby for something nonalcoholic.

"Who is this guy?" Arden asks as the girls race into the bedroom to play dress-up.

"He's really tall and cute," I say. "He's in AA, too."

"Why?" Arden asks.

"He's working on being sober, I guess."

Arden raises her eyebrows. "He's *working* on it?"

"It's a process," I say, repeating what Robby has said to me. "We're just going out for tea. Don't worry."

"Be careful," she says. (Isn't that what my sister told me, too? It seems like the word "sober" must bring up a lot for people.)

At the teahouse on College Avenue, Robby wants to tell me about AA's Twelve Steps. "But I want you to be in my arms when I explain this to you, okay?" he says. He props a few pillows against the wall, and I lean back into him.

"I'm working on my inventory of my past right now," he says. "That's Step Number Four."

"I could use some work on that, too," I say.

I'm not joking. I know that one of the reasons that dating still terrifies me is that I've screwed up with men in the past. I wish I could look back at all my mistakes fearlessly.

"I think we could help each other," he says, wrapping his arms around me.

"You do?" I take a deep breath.

"Yes," he whispers, bending down to kiss the top of my head.

"Come here," he says, pulling me toward him with his long arms.

"Is this one of the steps?" I giggle. He turns my face gently toward his. When we kiss, his mouth tastes like chai tea. He takes his time, not too much tongue. His bottom lip teases me for more. He's the kind of man who knows how to kiss—it's so underrated and such a turn-on.

The next night, after tucking Mae in, I call him. There's a recording on his phone: "We're sorry, but the number you're trying to reach is not in service." What? Has his phone been disconnected? I'm worried.

I send him an email: "Robby, are you okay? It's me . . ."

There's no reply. Was it something I said?

Four days later, there's a message on my voice mail. "I quit my waiting job," he says. "I'm behind in my bills, but I'll have phone service again soon." There's a siren in the background; he probably called from a pay phone.

I don't respond. A few days later, there's an email.

"I'd like to see you," he writes. "Want to come over this weekend?"

"I need to be with a man who can pay his bills," I write back.

"Harsh," he replies.

Robby is on his own journey now—aren't we all? I'm not sure if he has enough room for me. Or even if he's right for me.

So, I'm taking things one day at a time, as they say in AA. And that means deciding that Robby and I are not a good match after all.

■■■■■

A few days later, there's an email in my in-box that says "Literary Dada" in the subject line. *Very clever*, I think, knowing that this mystery man is responding to my Match.com username: "Literary Mama."

He doesn't stop there. He writes, "I am a warm and generous 30-year-old single dad who is seeking a respectful and cooperative woman who dreams with both feet on the ground, too!" He's still playing off my profile: "I am a warm and generous single mom seeking a respectful and cooperative man who dreams big with both feet on the ground. . . ."

I'm impressed. Here is a man who pays close attention to details.

When I click on his profile, Ronaldo seems to be looking right at me, his lips formed into a flirtatious smile. A six-foot-tall, Latino father of two, he's completing his dissertation in psychology at UC Berkeley. *Hmmm, a psychology major.* The skeptic in me wonders if this means he'll play mind games or manipulate me with psychological tricks.

I stop caring altogether about tricks when I scroll down to the second photo Ronaldo has posted. He has caramel skin, short black hair, defined cheekbones, and wire-rimmed glasses. I feel my cheeks flush as I sit in my T-shirt and panties shopping for a man on my computer. I go back and read his entire profile, the most specific and in-depth I've seen yet on Match.com. He says that he's looking for a confident, friendly, and passionate woman who can be in love with her partner and with life itself.

Brainy and bold women turn him on. *Well, that could work for me*, I think.

Then I read this line: "I don't really do things, I delegate them." I pause.

I delegate. What is he getting at? Is he good at giving orders and assigning tasks? Or is he raising his kids to be conscientious decision makers? Maybe he just means that he's very responsible and trustworthy? I feel a red flag coming on, but I decide to ignore it.

I continue reading. He writes that we can't always be happy-go-lucky and that "if you're having a crappy day, I hope I can bring you back to a place of balance." How thoughtful! I think.

He goes on to say that he enjoys simplicity—a glass of red wine, a soft kiss, and easy conversation.

So, who cares if he likes to give orders once in a while? In my own sometimes-chaotic and cluttered life, I could use a little delegation. I write back to Ronaldo, thanking him for the note.

"How could I resist?" he responds. "I would love to hear more about you! In fact, I'm looking forward to it incredibly!"

A week later, we're at the same cozy teahouse where I met Robby, sharing a pot of jasmine tea. As we swap life stories, I learn that he joined the army at age eighteen, married at age nineteen, and had two kids who are a year apart. His spouse was not happy being a military wife, and they often argued. She wanted to go to law school and moved to Washington, DC, to do so. They decided to get divorced, and he now has sole custody; the kids are with his ex every summer. I'm impressed by his devotion to his children and the fact that he's doing it on his own, like me.

Every time my teacup is almost empty, Ronaldo is right there, filling it up. "Thank you," I find myself saying over and over, touched by his attentiveness.

After our first meeting, we talk on the phone every night after our kids' bedtime. One night, he calls me at 8:15 sharp, after tucking his kids in. I can hear his voice on the answering machine in the other room: "Please call me."

But bedtime in our house is dragging on. It is 8:45, and I'm squeezed into Mae's bed next to her, finishing another chapter out loud in Beverly Cleary's *Ramona the Pest.* I silently reprimand myself for not being more stringent with the routines in our household.

C'mon now, I say to myself. *Can't you have an actual bedtime, just leave the room, and have the rest of the night to yourself?* But, truth be told, I'm into Ramona—one of my childhood favorites—just as much as Mae is. I love Ramona!

Ronaldo has sent me some photos of his beautiful son and daughter, ages nine and ten, and I find myself taking mental notes of the background in every picture: His kitchen counter is spotless, books are neatly lined up on the shelf, and wine bottles are stacked on a rack in his living room, divided by red and white. This is nothing like my house. I've always wanted to be that organized. I'm in awe. But I also feel apprehensive. Are we compatible? The red-flag alert is waving a bit higher now.

We make plans to see each other again. For some reason, I find myself using army lingo in my email: "Secured childcare for Saturday."

He's amused: "How military was that . . . you are too cute! All systems are a go here, too." Now I can really see it.

But that morning, his baby sitter calls in sick with the flu, so I suggest we get together for the afternoon at the Berkeley Marina—with all the kids—to fly kites. He offers to pick us up at home.

I know this is against every single-parent dating rule. I've been on only one date with this guy; it's too early to drag my three-year-old daughter into the mix. Selfishly, I don't want to call the date off. Ah, another rule broken!

"We're going to see one of Mama's special friends, honey," I tell Mae. "He has kids, too. We're going to fly kites."

When I get into his shiny black Jetta, the first thing I notice is that he is impeccably dressed—button-down shirt, khakis, and leather belt. I sigh. Sure, Mae and I are pulled together. We're both in calf-high pedal pushers and sweatshirts. But Ronaldo's daughter wears a flowery summer dress, obviously just ironed; his son has on a button-down shirt, too. In comparison to Ronaldo and his kids, we are sporting a very casual—and very Berkeley—look. This is an afternoon of kite flying, isn't it?

The second thing I notice is that the leather seats in his car are immaculate, in sharp contrast to the back seat of my Toyota, where an orange crayon has melted into the fabric and cookie crumbs are strewn everywhere. No empty water bottles roll under his seats, either. I breathe in the scent of sandalwood, not the permanent stench of little-kid urine that seems to inhabit my car.

"I'm hungry!" Mae whines as I strap her into the car seat.

Ronaldo's daughter giggles until her brother nudges her in the ribs. He's eyeing Mae like she's weird.

I fumble around in my backpack for a cracker, but Ronaldo says, "I'm sorry, we don't eat in my car."

I must look confused because he goes on to explain, as if I'm one of his children, "The car is for driving and talking. Eating is done at the table."

Is he busting me?

Then I feel a gentle jab in my ribs. "Relax!" Ronaldo tells me. I exhale, zip up my backpack, and tell Mae, "We'll be there soon, sweetie."

The truth is, sometimes I wish I had more rules. I don't mean to sound conventional, but setting limits just isn't my forte. Our home is based on everything feminine: Nurturing and taking care of others have always been my strong points. Caring for Mae is my strong point; laying down the law is not. Yes, a lot of my strengths and weaknesses seem to fall along stereotypical gender lines. But they are who I am.

Imagine how clean my own car would be if I didn't allow anyone to eat in it! Just yesterday, I found a line of ants crawling over the sticky straps of Mae's car seat. I won't win a Good Housekeeping Seal, but there's no lack of fun, or love, or estrogen for that matter, in our house of girls.

There is dead silence in the back seat as we drive down to the marina. I want so badly to blurt out something my mother would say, like, "Well, isn't this a beautiful day to fly a kite!" I'm relieved when I hear Ronaldo's daughter turn to Mae and ask, "Do you have any pets?"

"Just fish," Mae sighs. "But I really want an orange and white girl cat because I can't pet my fish."

"I'm allergic to cats," Ronaldo tells me in the front seat.

Oh, that's too bad, I think. I love cats.

At the marina, Mae quickly gives up kite flying in order to roll down the steep hillside. She begs me to join her, and we end up in a dizzy jumble at the bottom. There is grass in my mouth, and suddenly, I can't stop laughing. Our elbows are brown with dirt.

When I look up, Ronaldo is standing at the top of the hill, looking unsure. I can't tell if he's disapproving or sorry that he's missing out. "Let more string out!" he directs his son, who obediently unravels the kite.

An hour later, it's time to cram back into Ronaldo's car. In the parking lot, I'm doing my best to brush the grass off Mae's clothes; his children are already strapped into their seat belts. I slip off Mae's muddy sneakers and hold them on my lap for the ride home.

As we roll back through the city, Mae looks out the window. Suddenly, she blurts out a line from one of her favorite TV shows: "We were as pleased as punch!" I chuckle a lonesome laugh that seems to resonate by itself against the shiny seats. And I wonder if I can be with a man whose parenting style is so radically different from mine.

I'm not looking for someone who parents like I do, but he's got to complement me, at the very least. Sure, my life could use a better system of cleaning and organizing. But I like how messy our family is. I don't need a man to fix the parts of my life I don't like. He needs to like me for who I am.

If Ronaldo were in my life, I might be tidier and more efficient; but after today, I can tell that he's not right for us. When I look back at our lives ten years from now, I doubt I'll remember the dirt stains I couldn't scrub out of Mae's jeans. Instead, I will hold on to the two of us rolling down the hill, my head woozy, as Mae jumps up, screaming, "Let's do it again!"

I know I won't see Ronaldo again, and that suits me fine. I'm beginning to tire of the promise of Match.com, followed by the reality that is never as hopeful as the words on the screen. I've been on Match.com for almost three months now. I've been writing regularly to twenty men and have gone out with about half of them, mostly first dates that don't progress any further.

Online dating is a true night job. I keep a thick binder of all these men, our correspondence and their photos. After getting Mae to sleep, I flip through the pages and study each man's writing. Does he try to ask me out right away, even before getting to know me? Does he attempt to seduce me by email? Does he try to pull personal details out of me, such as where I live?

If he doesn't seem like a whacko—and appears to be child-friendly—I'll go for the phone call. I *always* talk on the phone with a man before meeting him. In just a ten-minute phone conversation, I can tell right away if he's a good listener. If I say, "It's getting really late, and I need my rest," I listen closely for his reply.

Does he say, "It was great talking to you, sleep well"? That's a good sign. He respects the fact that I'm a single mom, that I need to rest.

But what if he says, "C'mon, the night is young"? Then it's clear that he doesn't have a clue about how my life works.

My first dates usually take place during daylight, and *always* in a public place. I tell Siobhan or Arden where I'm going to be, and I call them afterward.

I'm dating more than I ever have in my life. But something is wrong with me. When I look at myself in the mirror, my face is pasty white. There are gray circles under my eyes. I'm not smiling anymore. I have hangnails. This is turning out to be a futile, nonpaying night job.

I haven't met anyone I really like. Maybe I should just give this all up.

Then Jim contacts me.

His first email is odd. "Are you my ex-girlfriend?" he asks. "She is my vision of physical beauty and you look identical to her.

Your profile has the same emotional temperament as her, as well as your dedication to your child and your sense of adventure."

I'm annoyed. "No, I'm not your ex," I write back.

"I don't have any thoughts of attempting to get back with her but I was a bit curious if you were actually her," he writes back.

What a pickup line, I think.

Still, I'm intrigued. He's forty-two, the father of an eight-year-old girl. He has an MBA in finance, dreadlocks, and pumped-up biceps.

"How does a guy like me get to know a woman like you?" he writes. "Damn you are all that and a bag of flaming-hot Cheetos—just too hot for words."

I'm smiling.

"No, really," he says. "You are gorgeous."

He's got me hooked. Moreover, he tells me that he loves to read, hike, watch good movies, and cook spicy food.

When he says, "My daughter is the greatest joy in my life," I'm all his.

He asks about Mae. Now I'm really a goner. Nothing is more flattering than for a man to ask about her. I write "She's a very likeable little girl, poised and articulate."

I ask how long he's been divorced.

"I am not actually divorced yet," he writes. "It's a long story." Red flag.

He tells me that although he and his wife split up in the late nineties, they never actually sat down to sign the divorce papers. They have shared custody, but they are still married.

"I hope this doesn't scare you away," he says.

It should scare me away. It really should. This red flag is so bright and big that it's almost blinding.

I should delete him right now. A "separated" man is carrying a lot of heavy baggage—his own suitcase, plus his wife's. I don't want to help him lug all these bags around, do I?

"I greatly appreciate your honesty about your divorce," I write. "I mean, the fact that you're *not* divorced. But going out with a married man does make me uncomfortable."

So, why then do I meet him for a first date?

Because he writes back to tell me that he and his ex are seeing a lawyer this week to get the ball rolling. It's time. And I guess I believe him. I'm also hungry for sex—I haven't slept with anyone for almost a year, since Tom the fish man. It's time.

I'm wearing what my friend Arden calls my "first-date skirt." I've had this glittery turquoise skirt for a few years now—Amanda sent it to me for my birthday—and I love all the rainbow sequins that sparkle around the edges. I also feel absolutely at ease in this skirt. As Arden has noticed, I seem to wear it on every first date I have. But it is starting to fray a bit at the edges.

When she first commented about my "first-date skirt," I laughed. Oh, isn't this hilarious! Arden had giggled and said, "Yeah, every woman should have a first-date skirt!" But now, I'm tired of the skirt. I'm tired of all these first dates. No wonder this skirt looks so worn out. I wish I could give it a break.

Maybe I need a break, too. I'm starting to fray as much as the skirt.

My cup of tea is not the only thing that's heating up on my first date with Jim at Café Roma.

Jim has long dreadlocks; I've always wanted to be with a man who has dreadlocks. Maybe it's this thing I have for Lenny

Kravitz. Maybe it's the fact that a man with dreads simply stands out, and I like the attention I get for being with him. When I look at a man with dreads, I see attitude, uniqueness, sex appeal.

Customers buzz past us with hot coffee and pastries, but I hardly notice them. Jim is leaning forward, those thick, sexy dreads falling over his shoulders.

"What's one of your biggest fears in a relationship?" he asks me.

"That's a bold question for a first date," I say.

But the truth is, this is exactly the kind of question *I* ask men on a first date nowadays. Now that I'm treating dating like a job. Now that I'm ready to be in an actual relationship. I'm realizing that to be in a fulfilling and meaningful relationship, I will have to work at it.

"I'm serious," he says, leaning his muscular forearms toward me.

"I'm afraid of trusting a man again," I say. "It's that simple."

When he nods his head, I feel like he understands.

"That reminds me," I say. "How's the divorce going?"

"It's messy right now. We're still hammering out the custody deal."

"Hammering out?" I say.

"The hammers are pounding quite loudly right now," he says.

I nod my head. But I'm not buying it. Jim is still a married man and it could be a long time until he's not. Time for me to leave. But I don't. Am I that naive? Or just hungry for some hot sex with a dreadlocked man? As I wrap my fingers around the warm paper cup, I imagine wrapping them around something else. I guess I have my answer.

At the end of our first date, we stand up and he wraps his arms around me. His hair smells like coconut. I want more of him, red flag or no.

When I get home, there's an email from him: "I want to hold my breath because I feel like any moment now I'll wake up and see that it is just a dream. I can't even concentrate. I don't mean to put any pressure on you, but I am really happy we have met."

Damn, it's hard to turn this down. *So what if he hasn't signed his divorce papers? What's the big deal?* But at the same time I'm thinking this, another faint voice—the voice of reason—tells me I should call it off. But reason is no match for some serious sexual chemistry.

On our second date, we meet at the Berkeley Marina for a walk. When we turn the corner to walk up a narrow path, I let him lead the way. Instead of watching his dreads, I keep my eyes on his cute ass. When I catch up with him, our hands brush against each other. I keep waiting for him to touch me. For some reason, I'm nervous about making the first move. It's so unlike me. Typically, I have no problem being assertive.

But dating as a single mom is so strange. Now that I have a daughter, I'm afraid of making a wrong move. My heart is pounding. Is it excitement? Adrenaline? All the walking uphill? This feeling is so familiar; I've wrongly followed it before, confusing my jumpiness for love. I don't want that to happen again.

Jim asks if I took the Match.com personality test online. I started to fill out the questions, I tell him. But they were kind of ridiculous.

"Well, my results said that I have a higher sex drive than most," he says.

"Oh, really?" I stop walking. He stops, too. He lifts his hand and strokes my cheek. "You're gorgeous," he says.

We keep walking. We cover a wide range of topics that are close to my heart: our kids, which books we're reading right now, where we plan to travel next. Jim tells me about making dinner for his daughter the night before: spicy chicken, broccoli stir-fry, and corn bread. As he talks, I put myself and my own child right there, in his living room, the four of us eating together. As usual, I'm putting the cart before the horse.

We hug each for a long time at the end of our walk. I press my face into his dreads. I imagine dreading my own hair someday, as well as my daughter's. We'll be a multicultural, devoted, dreadhead family.

Siobhan and Arden will think I'm nuts. Maybe I am nuts.

Back at home, there's another email from Jim: "My stomach is in knots. I wanted to grab you, hug, squeeze, and caress and kiss you—you are awesome! You are the bomb! I really want to hold you, hug you, caress you, kiss you, love and make love to you."

Hmmm, this seems a little bit fast, even for me.

Over the next few weeks, Jim and I get to know each other—well. We meet at the park for lunch to make out in the grass. I follow him home after hearing jazz one night and stretch out on his sofa. He tells me that he wants to gobble up my breasts.

"Oh no!" I cover myself up with my hands. "They're still very sensitive from all that nursing."

"I'll be gentle," he says, pulling me on top of him.

I am almost businesslike the way I prepare for the real thing. Did you get your HIV test? Check! Is my birth control prescription ready? Check!

A few days later, I know it's going to happen.

Siobhan offers to take Mae, who's almost four, for a sleepover. This is her very first all-nighter away from me. Most kids her age don't do overnights yet. But then, most kids her age have two parents. I know that Mae will be fine with Siobhan and her daughter, Hazel. Siobhan is like the big sister I never had. Still, I worry that Mae will wake up crying for me.

When we arrive, Siobhan is stirring a pot of mac and cheese—Mae's favorite food—as Hazel brushes her Barbie's hair on the kitchen floor. Of course, Siobhan has feathers sticking out of her hair and mismatched plaid socks on her feet. If I were a kid, I'd love hanging out with Siobhan.

"Mae Mae!" Siobhan greets my daughter by her nickname.

Mae clings to my leg.

"Do you know what we're having for dessert tonight? Ice cream sundaes!"

"Sundaes!" Hazel jumps up from the floor.

But Mae pulls on my skirt. "Don't go, Mommy!"

"I'll be back—"

"No!" Here come the instant tears. Why does she have to be so dramatic? Like mother, like daughter.

Siobhan leaves the pot on the stove and bends down next to Mae, rubbing her back. "Sweetheart, we're going to have so much fun! We're going to watch *Cinderella*—"

"*Cinderella* scares me!" Mae screams.

"Okay, then, we'll pick out another video," Siobhan says.

Then she turns to me and waves toward the door: "Go!"

Go? And leave her in tears? But Jim is waiting for me. He'll be at my place any minute now.

On the ten-minute drive home, I almost dial Jim's phone number to call it off. My own eyes are welling up with tears. *It's okay if she cries a little. Tears are healthy, right? She's in good hands.*

The closer I get to home, the smugger I get. *It's about time I get a break! I deserve this. Don't I get one night off from being Mom?*

I also try to replace images of Mae in tears with ones of Jim seducing me. I think about his dreadlocks and his pumped-up biceps. I remember how gently he held my face when he kissed me. Back at home, I slip on my pink see-through lingerie under my dress. I turn the phone and lights off. I light some candles.

There's a knock at the door.

I fly down the stairs with a big smile. This is it! This is my night. It's my chance to forget about the week-old milk in the fridge, the dishes coated with macaroni and cheese, the Barbie shoes strewn across the rug, and the unbalanced checkbook. I am going to let myself go.

Jim comes inside, and we waste no time. Our clothes quickly fall to the floor. My world is wet and wide open.

But just ten minutes and not many thrusts later, there's a loud groan. His head hits the pillow. His eyes are shut.

"What about me?" I say.

"*Hmmm?*" he says.

I shake his shoulder. "What about me?"

The next morning when I show up at Siobhan's, there are dark circles under her eyes.

"Are you okay?" I ask. (I know *I'm* not.)

"She cried until midnight," Siobhan says. "But don't worry, I held her and told her that I loved her."

I bite my bottom lip. I've just traumatized my little girl, and I didn't even get an orgasm out of it. Siobhan wants a full report. I tell her the disappointing details. She reminds me: "Sex is a process. You've got to work on it."

Maybe she's right.

Over the next few months, Jim and I continue to meet for some late-night fooling around. I try to guide him to relax and slow down. Part of the problem seems mechanical: He's moving so fast that he's not really present with me. His hard-on directs the show: Sex becomes an overexcited monologue, instead of both of us playing complementary parts on stage.

"No other woman has ever complained," he says. I think I actually gasp in surprise. He must be joking. In any case, I see a red flag out of the corner of my eye, or rather staring me in the face.

But I am not trying to damage his male ego. All I need is ten minutes, only ten minutes before he lets the dam burst. Yet, time and time again, just when I am ready to go over the edge, he is gone.

I hold tightly to my fantasies. I want to yell his name out loud as my body shudders. I want to feel his sweat roll off me. But it's not just about sex. I imagine blending our families together one day, and buying a house with a backyard swing and a huge playroom. But I know that's not going to happen as long as I remain chronically unsatisfied.

One afternoon when I'm home alone, I strip off my clothes and set up my digital camera to take some naked photos on the self-timer. I draft an email to Jim as if I'm his boss. I ask him to please complete this important assignment: "Please refer to the attached and masturbate as often as possible. You can do this right from your computer. Or you can print them out and find a quiet spot all to yourself. Imagination is a big plus here. (Of course, I'm willing and open to participate in any work sessions, but due to time constraints that is not always possible.) This is all guaranteed to improve your stamina."

He writes back, "Oh my God! They say you have to watch out for the quiet ones, and I now know that they were right. You are so hot. . . . You are something else . . . do you know that! Okay, time to get to work. As you know I have a BIG job in front of me."

Still, each week, Jim comes over, and boy, does he come. I don't. My fantasies are flooded by fury. Yet, I can see that he's working on it. I'm also in deep. That's because Mae is in the big picture, too. He recently invited us over for dinner and served us his spicy chicken. I had seconds. Afterward, his daughter taught Mae magic tricks, and they put on a show.

Then one night, three months into our relationship, it happens. He comes over after Mae is asleep and crashes hard in my bed. In the middle of the night, when he's half-asleep, I climb on top of him. Perhaps this makes for less pressure to perform. Perhaps it's just luck. He hardly moves, but I sure do. I actually climax. In that moment, every doubt I had disappears into the darkness. I want to marry him on a mountaintop. I want us to take a bow together. But is this really a solution?

Meanwhile, Jim never makes another move to finalize his divorce. He goes on and on about child-support payments and the fact that his wife makes more money. I know what this means: A man with unfinished business is not really complete. Part of him is still with his wife. I've had just a glimpse of the other part of him, and it's not of much use to me right now. But true to form, I think I can change him—I'm on a mission.

I invite Jim over every weekend now, eager to repeat our performance. But time and time again, he is coming fast. I am running high on frustration. The very last time, as soon as he started to snore, I was out of bed, on my knees picking up Barbie accessories from the rug. When that last plastic high heel was put away, I knew this was over.

Chapter Seven: Offline, and Back to Reality

Forget about online dating. Jim and I break up, and I take myself offline. I am tired of trying to find a man on the computer. Siobhan is right: I've got to smell a man. I just want to have some good sex right now, so I've gone back to the old-fashioned way of looking for a real, live man in the flesh.

I'm a good mom, but I also have some bad-girl moments.

The fourth floor of the Holiday Inn Pleasant Hill reeks of old cigarette smoke. The deep voice of a TV newscaster seeps under a door into the empty hallway. I've emptied my backpack of cracker crumbs and crayons for everything I need tonight: my toothbrush, a pair of Levi's, clean underwear, and condoms. I've also brought along some food to accompany the wine that I look forward to sipping. I'm just a few miles from where I grew up in these conventional suburbs.

But at this moment, I'm so far from anything conventional. I'm a good mom, but I'm also a bad girl. My bad girl—the part of me that exists despite all the responsibilities, tasks, and pressures of single motherhood—hasn't emerged in a long time. She's *not* exactly bad. She's this part of me that wants so badly to do things that might be out of character. She makes her most dramatic appearances when I'm feeling out of control with balancing the demands of the rest of my life. To be honest, I'm also on the rebound.

When I lift my hand to knock on the door, the grimy numbers "404" remind me of something a computer programmer ex-boyfriend once told me. When the Internet was still text-based, an ambitious group of scientists worked day and night to create the World Wide Web in an office in Switzerland. Legend has it that their central database was located in Room 404, so any request for a file from that database was routed to Room 404. If someone requested a file by the wrong name, they'd get the standard message: "Room 404: file not found." To this day, that message still appears if you make an error on the computer.

This bad girl is not afraid of making errors. She has been around since I was a teenager—but I've kept a tight lid on her since becoming a mom.

Not anymore.

The only way to calm myself down during a period of intense restlessness is to seek a man I don't know very well and live for the moment: This is how I end up in Room 404 of the Holiday Inn with Conner. Room 404. Does this mean I'm making a mistake?

When Conner opens the door, all my doubts vanish. He's wearing a white, flowing cotton shirt with all the top buttons undone and loose-fitting cotton pants. I smile at him and think, *You're my angel.*

"Hi," I whisper. My voice is shy.

When I step into the dark room, I expect him to kiss me or embrace me. But he turns off the TV, sits down on the edge of the bed, and lights a cigarette. We don't say a word, but I'm smiling. I step over to the coffee table and pull my picnic supplies out of their brown bag, setting them up on the paper plates I've also packed. There are sweet purple grapes, fancy salted crackers, and cheddar cheese. I even brought along a knife and a small, plastic cutting board to chop a green apple into small, perfect slices. My routine comes effortlessly. This is so easy, in fact, that I almost forget I'm making a snack for a sexy, grown man who's ready to make love to me. Silly me, I'm so used to cutting everything into bite-size pieces for my four-year-old daughter!

"This is weird," Conner says.

"What is?"

"Everything. You don't just go to a hotel room with someone you don't know and have a picnic."

I hold the knife in midair. You don't? Why not? Isn't this every man's dream, to have an attractive woman he hardly knows spend the night with him at a random hotel?

Maybe this was all a very bad idea. Maybe I should just turn around and go home.

Somewhere in the back of my mind, Siobhan is talking to me. *What on earth are you doing, Rachel? What if he's a serial killer? What if he has a disease? Is it really worth it?*

I push those thoughts away and sit on the bed, close to Conner but not touching. I'm *not* willing to give up the possibility of a wild night this easily. Conner is looking down at my thighs, which peek out of my tight jean skirt. I shaved my legs during a quick shower this afternoon, as my daughter played dolls in her room, and the lotion makes them gleam. I nervously clasp my hands in front of me.

"It's all going to be okay," I say to Conner, raising my voice in a sweet inflection. This is exactly what I often say to my kid when she resists doing something, like going to the dentist. Goodness, the transition from mom to bad girl is a little tougher than I thought.

I barely know Conner—we've been on only one date. Going back to my place with a new man is *not* an option. Likewise, going back to his place could be unsafe. Personally, I like to get creative in neutral spots, like a hotel room.

"Want some wine?" Conner says, offering me his glass.

That's when I notice the bottle of white wine on the bedside table, already opened. I take a very long swig, emptying the glass. My hunger for him and the bad girl in me both come out in full force.

A few Sundays ago, Conner and I meet while I'm shopping for a bed frame, and my sister is hanging out with Mae. Yes, how fitting to meet him there, given my frame of mind.

Mae and I have been sleeping together on a mattress and box spring since she was born. At first, it was a practical convenience to share a bed. But now that I'm dating, it is time for her to move to her own bed. She is no longer nursing, and her nighttime thrashing often wakes me up. I score a half-price deal on the floor model of a castle bed for her, complete with two towers and real turrets. It even comes with a real slide that starts under one of the towers.

This is a dream-come-true for both of us. She can sleep like a princess, and I get a full night's rest. Just imagine all the wild things I can do in my very own bed! I can fantasize undisturbed. I can even masturbate in peace.

Still, there's something humbling about sleeping on a mattress on the floor while your daughter sleeps in a princess bed. She is not oblivious to this supremacy. One of her favorite games is dress-up. She loves to come out in a glittery gown and say, "Okay, Mom, you're the servant!"

She hands me the broom.

"Can't I be the queen?" I say.

"No!" she says. "Now find my crown!"

So, the afternoon I go out alone to buy myself a real bed frame feels like a big deal. At thirty-two, I think it's time.

I first see Conner behind the counter, with his back to me. He is at least six feet tall, and his head is shaved. I have this thing for men who are bald. When I see him—his smooth head beautifully shaped—I want to reach out and wrap my hands around it.

He turns around, and I see that he has big, deep brown eyes and one of those open faces you just want to tell your life story to.

"Hi. Can I help you?" His voice is deep and smooth, and his soft eyes look straight into mine.

"I'm just fine, thanks!" I say a bit too enthusiastically. But I'm not just fine. I'm red. I have this tendency to blush madly when I'm embarrassed or, as the case may be, terrifically attracted to someone.

My hands are hot, and I pretend to read the price tags: $115, $225, $400. My mind is a blank. What size mattress do I have again?

"Let me know if you need my help . . ."

There he is, right behind me. All the bed frames around me blur together, and I stop breathing as I browse.

Focus! I command myself. *Don't forget what you're here for!* But my mission has changed. What am I here for again? A mattress? Or a man?

I turn another corner, sure that our eyes will lock again, but he is gone. Is he back at the front counter? No. Maybe he darted into the kids' department? Damn!

I turn yet another corner, and there he is, laid out in a big bed with his hands behind his neck. His shiny black boots are on the plastic-covered mattress.

He sits up and offers me his hand. "Hi."

I grip his fingers and let him pull me right onto that bed. That's when I notice his tag: "Manager." Certainly, this is a man in charge.

"Do you always sleep on the job like this?" I ask.

"Whenever I get the chance."

I laugh. We lie there staring at each other. Finally, he says, "You came on the right day. It's our biggest sale of the year, and I'm going to give you a deal."

"Yeah?"

"Yeah," he says. "I like you."

I smile, and my limbs go limp.

"I like you so much," he continues, "that I'm losing my focus . . ."

"Me, too!"

He sits up and tells me that I can take this very bed home for just $299, with a matching bedside table thrown in free. I run my hand over the all-silver frame; this is my favorite metal. The headboard has long, wavy curves with three teardrops in the middle. I love its strength and sensuality. The fact that Mr. Hot sits in this very bed also makes the deal quite appealing.

A week after meeting Conner at the bed store, we go on a date to an outdoor bar in downtown Berkeley. We sit across from each other and sip white wine as the outdoor heat lamps beam down on us. Conner tries to talk above the live music onstage, and I lean across the table to hear him.

"I have to be straight with you," he tells me, explaining that he and his girlfriend of three years have just broken up, and he is moving out. He's on the rebound; they'll probably get back together. Major red flag. I close my eyes for a moment, knowing this will never go anywhere.

Conner is just a flirt, I think. *But hey, what do I think* I'm *doing?*

"So, I guess that means I can't come home with you tonight?" I tease.

Conner sits up straight, looking both excited and nervous. "Well, uh—"

I giggle. I just want to get a reaction from him.

I push my artichoke-spinach dip across the table and ask if he wants to try some. He picks up the ceramic bowl, smells it, and puts it down.

"No thanks." He scrunches up his face.

"You didn't just smell my food, did you?" I ask.

"So?"

"That's exactly what my daughter does before she takes a bite of anything new," I say. "Then she usually does just what you did: She pushes it away like that."

As I talk about her, I miss her terribly, and when I get like that I can't stop talking. "Let me show you a photo," I say, reaching for my wallet. I hand him a recent black-and-white picture, and he studies it in the dim light. "She's beautiful."

At the end of our date, Conner walks me to my car and wraps his arms around me. I close my eyes, blocking out the bright yellow streetlight. The Bay Area fog wraps around the city, but I hardly feel it. I try to hold on to thoughts of my daughter, of safety and responsibility; I have to get into my car to relieve my friend of baby-sitting duties, but this hug pulls me back. Nothing in the world matters right now except being held.

This is when I propose that we meet next Saturday at a hotel, and he readily agrees. Looking back, I don't know what I was thinking. That night, he makes reservations and emails that he'll be waiting for me at six. At home, I get Mae to sleep, and then the bad girl in me gets pushy. *What's wrong with a one-night stand? Use protection, tell your girlfriends where you're going, and be safe.* I want to embrace that bad girl for now, even if I tell her to go to hell in the morning.

I call Arden to tell her my plans, and send an email with all the stats: hotel address and phone number. I add, "Don't worry, I got condoms, too."

Arden writes back: "Just be sure to listen to yourself if you are feeling uncomfortable or whatever! Have fun."

I can't bring myself to tell Siobhan. Surely, she'll say, "He might be a serial killer."

Surely then, I would chicken out. I decide to tell her postcoitus.

***

This is supposed to be perfect. In Room 404, there is no daughter needing her hair washed and combed, no baked potatoes that need buttering, no parent-teacher conference to prepare for, no dishes to clean in the sink. It is simple: just me, my man, and one big bed. The shades are closed; we have total privacy. In case we get hungry, our picnic is spread out.

I strip. Since giving birth, I have absolutely no qualms about being naked. My stretch marks are a badge of honor and pride, not something to be embarrassed about.

When I fall back on the bed, Conner lies next to me, still dressed. He reaches out and strokes my hair. *What's he waiting for? C'mon!* I reach out and tug on his cotton pants. My fingers move under the elastic and skim his dark skin.

"Stop!" he says, uncertainly. "You're tickling me."

He stands up and turns off the bedside lamp. In the darkness, he slides out of his pants and lies down next to me. His shyness amuses me.

"How about your shirt?" I ask, fingering a white button.

"I don't want you to see my chest."

"Why not?" I ask.

"I don't work out like I used to."

"So? You're gorgeous!"

I unbutton the button.

"No, really," he says.

"C'mon, Conner, if anyone should be embarrassed about her chest, it's me! *I'm* the one who breastfed for almost three years."

He takes a deep breath and pulls his shirt over his head. I crawl on top of him and lick his nipples. "*Mmmm,* nice," I hum, working my way down his tense belly to his cotton briefs.

Feeling how nervous he is only makes me more excited. I gently kiss him above the elastic. He moans. I slowly pull off his underwear and roll a condom on his hard, long dick. I climb back on to his lean body, breathing us in. This is it. When I look into his eyes and see how focused he is—on me—I'm in control. I move my hips, and he gently takes hold of me. I devour this attention. He hits my G-spot, and I groan. I come quickly.

When he slides out of me, I'm surprised. Is that it? He pulls the condom off with a snap and grips my hips, drawing me on to my back. He's over me, entering me suddenly, the tip of his dick. We're unprotected. I freeze.

"Don't," I say, vulnerably.

"Please," he says. "I just want to feel you, just for a second."

Our connection is so strong: We're playing that childhood game of looking into each other's eyes, neither of us blinking, just holding on for as long as possible. I don't want to let go of this, I don't want to lose this.

His cell phone is ringing on the table.

I jump away. He reaches out to answer his phone.

"I can't talk right now, baby," he says. "No, everything's fine, I'm just finishing some business here. I'll call you back soon." A red flag is now waving slowly and ominously over my face.

I have no doubt that he's talking to his "ex-" girlfriend.

When I sit up, the mother in me is back. Making a snack feels so ordinary. I slice cheese on the tiny hotel table. I try to hold on to that feeling of both of us so connected: his fingers pressing the small of my back, mine wrapped around his smooth head.

But as I move away from him, a voice inside me says, *Now look at what you've done. What the hell were you thinking? Unprotected sex? You might die.*

This reprimanding voice is familiar. Is it my Catholic mother, descended from a long line of women who tried to do well by the church but often failed? Or is it my well-meaning, protective soul sister, Siobhan? The voice is treating me like a child, judging me for my wrongdoing. My mind goes straight to self-loathing, as the voice scorns this bad girl in the worst way.

On my way home, desperation washes over me, and when I climb the stairs, there's my new silver bed frame with its matching table.

Just because my daughter and I sleep in our super-cool separate beds now, I don't exactly have privacy. My "bedroom" is half the living room. There is no door. It's a challenge trying to keep my private life under wraps.

During the mad rush to get five-year-old Mae to preschool this morning, I duck my head into the bathroom and command for the fourth time, "Please brush your teeth!"

"Mommy, what's this?" she asks.

In her little closed fist is a Trojan Condom, still smartly packaged in gold, glittering in the morning light like a party favor she brought home from a friend's birthday party.

Damn.

"Nothing!" I snatch the rubber from her. "We're late for school!"

"But I want to open it," she says.

White toothpaste encircles her lips. Her hair is in pigtails. She seems pure and innocent.

"No!" I say. "C'mon, let's go!"

Normally, my sex supplies—condoms, birth control pills, vibrator—are stashed on the highest shelf in our bathroom, above the deodorant, aloe vera, and Band-Aids. But this wayward condom must have jumped off its shelf and landed on the floor.

I wish I could say that I stood still at this very moment and thought, *Who cares if we're five minutes late for school? Talking to my daughter is more important.*

I wish I could say that I seized this opportunity to give my daughter an age-appropriate lesson on safe sex. I wish I could say that I am the kind of mother who has no qualms about showing her child what a condom is.

But this morning, I say none of these things. Instead, I grab her jacket, dash down the stairs, and remind her, "It's pizza day!"

There, that's easy. We've moved on from safe sex to pizza.

More important, the condom is back in its place and forgotten.

Still, after kissing Mae goodbye at school, my conscience starts speaking to me, as it often does. *She's just curious, that's all.*

I remember the look of disappointment on her face as I seized the evidence. Why did I react so crossly, as if she'd done something wrong? She's only five years old! That wasn't right. *Oh, my baby, I'm sorry.*

Haven't I always vowed to teach her that no subject is off-limits, that she can talk to me about anything? We live in Berkeley, for heaven's sake! I grew up in the suburbs with a Catholic mother who never uttered the word "sex," and the last thing I want is for Mae to feel condemned. Don't I want her to be educated and informed? Yes, she should go into this world knowing how to take care of her body.

What am I so afraid of?

Mae knows exactly what a penis and vagina are. In fact, one of her favorite books is *Mommy Laid an Egg: Or, Where Do Babies Come From?* by Babette Cole, an ironic story about a sophisticated brother and sister who must explain reproduction to their nervous, afraid parents. Mae laughs when the parents try to explain that babies are made out of gingerbread or squeezed out of a tube.

The book has created a stir among some parents, who claim, for instance, that drawings of couples having sexual intercourse on a skateboard or suspended in the air by helium balloons are lewd and inaccurate. It has been banned from many libraries.

I've read this book to her over and over. So, why can't I just sit down and tell her what a rubber is? What am I so afraid of?

It's this: What if my daughter asks me if I have sex? What would I say to her? *Yes, Mommy has sex. Didn't you wonder why you sometimes go to a friend's house for a sleepover? I've even had sex when you're fast asleep in your big-girl bed in the next room. I sometimes worry that you'll wake up when you hear the bed squeaking. I can make an awful racket! I'm glad that you're finally a deep sleeper.* I don't think so. We'll postpone this conversation for later.

Tonight, Mae and I are back in the bathroom, brushing our teeth before bed. She's wearing her Disney Princess nightgown and Dora the Explorer slippers. She looks so wholesome.

But I can't stand it anymore. I open the cupboard, reach up, and pull the condom down from its spot on the shelf. I hadn't realized that it's an "extra-large," a freebie I grabbed after a recent doctor's appointment. This is going to be worse than I'd imagined. I take a deep breath.

"Remember this?" I ask.

She nods her head.

"I'm sorry about this morning, when you asked me what this was, and I didn't explain it. I'm going to tell you now, okay?"

She puts her toothbrush down on the counter. Her face is eager and open. I bend down so that we're face to face. I begin by reminding her how babies are made, like in the book *Mommy Laid an Egg*. As I talk, I rip open the package. Her eyes are glued to it.

"This is called a condom," I say, pulling it out. She reaches out and touches the latex.

"Remember that a man has little seeds inside him that come out? Well, this traps the seeds so they can't get into a woman's body and make a baby."

She pulls hard on the latex. "They get stuck in here?"

"That's right, honey." She lets go, and it snaps in the air.

"But, Mommy, why don't you want to have another baby?"

"Another baby?"

"Yes, I want a baby sister."

Whew, this is going to be a breeze. I list all the reasons I'm not going to have another baby right now, like the fact that we live in a one-bedroom apartment that is too small for another baby, and the fact that babies cost a lot of money. I skirt around my relationship status.

"Most of all," I say, "I'm so happy with you right now, my big girl."

Then she dashes out the door to choose her bedtime story from the shelf. I grab a wad of toilet paper and wrap it around the wasted condom. Well, it wasn't exactly wasted. It did go to a good cause, right?

Alone in the bathroom, I say a silent prayer to myself: *Please, Mae, don't tell your friends or your teacher about this. Please.*

Tucked under her covers, Mae seems satisfied. I'm relieved that she wants me to read a cute picture book about a mischievous kitten. We've both had enough of all that sober sex-talk.

However, after tiptoeing out of her room, I remember that the bathroom is not the only spot where I stash sex supplies. Under my bed for the past couple of weeks, I've been collecting free samples of all-natural lubricants for a stylish product inventory article I'm writing for *Tango* magazine. I've been mailed about twenty different varieties, chemical-free and in every flavor from cinnamon to berry.

Unfortunately, Mae had intercepted the postman earlier this week. "Is it for me?" she asked, jumping up and down, as he handed me a plain brown package. "Is it? Is it?"

"Uh—"

"What is it, Mommy?"

I let her open the box, explaining that there are some "special lotions" inside. She squeezed some strawberry-mango O'My Lubricant out of the bottle and rubbed it on her forearm.

"It smells good," she said. "But it's sticky."

Oh, no. I'm not yet ready to explain the word "lubricate" to her.

As Mae gets older, I realize that she might learn some things sooner with a single parent. After all, we're so close. We're in constant proximity. Our home is all about estrogen and girl-power.

As much as I'm looking for Mr. Right, I love hanging out with my kid. We have fun together. On Friday nights, we pick up a pizza and watch a movie. Her favorite right now is *Toy Story,* which happens to feature a single-parent family.

This Friday night, I'm waiting for a take-out pizza at Zachary's on Solano Avenue. Mae is unpeeling a big sticker that the nice waiter just gave her and attaching it to my butt. I ignore her.

That's because I'm peering over the counter at all the couples eating out together. What I would do right now to be part of a pair having a romantic dinner.

Actually, having my daughter there, too, would be just fine. All I want is someone to share a deep-dish pizza with me. Of course, this someone would have to be male—and capable of conversation as deep as the pizza. What I would do for a Chicago-style deep-dish right now, all that red chunky tomato sauce oozing out, with mushrooms and spinach hiding under the cheese.

But Mae will eat only the thin crust—and *only* cheese. Since it's just the two of us and I'm watching my budget, thin crust it is.

When I turn my head, I see him.

Adam. Even though it's been almost three years, he made quite an impression. There he is at the corner table next to the window, taking a bite of deep-dish pizza. His two preteen daughters sit across from him. His older daughter hands him a napkin, and he wipes a string of cheese from his chin.

I've met Adam only once, back when Mae and I had just moved back to Berkeley. My landlord, who lives below us, invited us over for some cookies. I'd spent an exhausting day moving and felt sweaty and in need of a shower. But we were only going downstairs to have a snack with Zoë, our landlord's eleven-year-old daughter. Two-year-old Mae was thrilled to be living in the same house as a true big girl. Zoë even had a friend over that day, so Mae was in girly heaven.

"Want to play?" they asked Mae when we walked in.

Mae jumped into a game of Groovy Girls dolls, as I stretched out on the rug with some ice water. Just then, the doorbell rang.

That was when I first saw Adam, and of course the first thing I noticed was his shaved head, one of my major turn-ons. He was carrying a black motorcycle helmet. He smiled at me as he leaned against the doorway, quiet, giving off that bad-boy energy that always draws me right in.

"Hi Daddy!" my neighbor's friend said.

"Hey, baby," he said.

No way! This guy was a father?

I wiped a sweaty wisp of hair away from my temple and stared at my white knees clearly visible in my cut-off Levi's. Why hadn't I taken a shower? Why is it that I tend to meet cute and possibly even available men when I'm in my grungy clothes or just leaving the gym at the YMCA?

Thank goodness my landlord walked in just then. "Were you on duty last night?" she asked him.

"Another night of chasing drug dealers," he said. "But that's life on the San Francisco beat."

I thought, *I wouldn't mind being chased by you!*

She introduced us: "This is Rachel. She just moved in upstairs."

I should have stood up to shake his hand. I should have said something intelligent like, "Does your daughter ever baby-sit? She's a great kid!"

Or maybe even something amusing, like, "I'm a reporter, and I'd like to do an investigative piece about a local cop."

But I just squeaked out a shy "Hello."

When he left, my landlord whispered to me, "You might like him. His ex-wife abandoned him, too."

Sure, I might have liked him. But back then, I was still fresh off the boat from New York, the new kid on the block. More than that, I was still getting over my ex. And I still had a complex about being a single mom.

I walked around staring at the ground, insecure and needy. I didn't know if I'd ever be in a relationship again, or even what I wanted that to look like. I certainly didn't have the guts to chat with a guy like Adam. But I wanted to, especially if I had on something more, well, sexy and confidence-inspiring.

Unlike most of the men I dated, Adam was at least ten years older than I, a homeowner, and the single father of two girls. I was sure that we'd run into each other in Berkeley. This is such a small town and he lives only a mile away from us. But in the intervening years it never happened.

Until now.

When Adam looks up from his pizza, I'm looking right at him.

He smiles. I smile back.

Does he remember me? I should walk up to him. I should say, "Hey, great to see you again!" But I'm flustered. He's with his daughters. I'm with mine.

When I get home, I can't stop thinking about him.

After getting Mae to sleep, I call my landlord downstairs and ask her straight out for Adam's phone number.

When I dial, my fingers are shaking.

"Hi, Adam, this is Rachel," I say, my voice cracking. "Uh, I hope I'm not calling you too late."

"No, but I don't know who you are," he says. His tone is uptight, cop-like.

"This is Rachel," I try again. "My landlord's daughter is friends with your daughter."

Silence.

"We met at Zachary's Pizza tonight," I try again.

"Zachary's?" he says. His voice is mean now. "I don't think so—"

I close my eyes. He doesn't know who the hell I am. I should hang up now. I've completely humiliated myself.

I take a deep breath. "Let me start again," I say. "In 2002, I'd just moved to Berkeley. I was unpacking when you came to my landlord's—"

"Oh!" he says. "What a nice surprise!"

The sudden warmth gives me the courage to keep talking. "So, tonight, I saw you at Zachary's but I was too shy to come over."

"Well, it took a lot of guts for you to call me like this," he says.

"Yeah," I agree.

"We should get together sometime," he says.

"Really?" I say. But I'm not breathing. *Yes! Yes! Yes!*

"What are you doing tomorrow night?" he asks.

"Tomorrow?"

"My daughters are in a play at the JCC. Want to come?"

"The JCC?" I say. "The Berkeley-Richmond Jewish Community Center? That's where my daughter goes to preschool."

It turns out that his daughters are in the after-school program there, on the opposite side of the building. It's unbelievable that we've never run into each other before.

It's also ironic that now, at age thirty-two, I have my first date with a Jewish man. Like me, Adam is culturally Jewish, but not observant. Yes, my very first date with a Jewish man in my whole life, unless you count junior high school.

I've been thinking a lot about Jewish men lately. That's because I'm surrounded by all these fun, gentle, warm Jewish fathers at Mae's preschool. I've observed them for over two years now—these genuine, big-hearted guys who dole out love to their kids and wives. Hey, I want one of those!

The play is in the same auditorium where Mae's preschool Shabbat dinners are held. This is precisely where, every few months without fail, I've found myself quietly studying the fathers of Mae's friends.

Two Fridays ago, in fact, Mae and I arrived for a Shabbat potluck dinner with a warm bowl of mac and cheese. Mae bounced in and grabbed a seat in between two cute dads. I said hello and squeezed in across from her.

A pang of envy hit me. Why can't I have a man like one of them?

There was Warren, the silliest dad in Mae's class, throwing his daughter into the air as she shrieked with joy. During the blessing over challah, Josh rested his hand on top of his son's.

I wanted a partner, too. An equal, a helper, a companion. Yes, a husband, even. Why did this envy have to sneak up on me now, smack in the middle of a school potluck dinner?

I watched as Warren put one arm around the back of his wife's chair and, with his other, offered his daughter another bite of pizza. As these dads doled out love to their kids and wives, I sat unaided, trying to persuade Mae to please take one little bite of rice.

"No!" she said, jumping out of her chair.

"Please," I asked.

"You're annoying me!" she said, and with that, she was gone, leaving me alone among all these two-parent families. I could feel myself sinking in resentment and anger. *C'mon now, Rachel, pull yourself out of it.*

I was idolizing these loving dads, parking myself in that negative place of pity, where all I could see was the "single" in "single parenthood."

And not only that, I'm not even technically Jewish. My dad is Jewish; my mom isn't. But my friends who are married to Jewish men seem blissfully happy. Plus, my close girlfriends, Siobhan and Arden, are both Jewish, and I adore them. So, where are the nice Jewish men? Siobhan and Arden have put their thinking caps on about this one.

"It only takes one good man to penetrate the true cockles buried in our hearts," says the ever-philosophical Siobhan. "Of course, we also need a barrel of humor to brighten our artistic loads, a dollop of compassion for our multitaskin' minds, a bucket of admiration, and a pinch of kinky!"

We all root for Siobhan, who's certain she'll meet her next man as they're standing over three pounds of artichokes at the local farmers market, where, she tells me, after smelling each other, they will go home and cook together.

As I sit at the potluck, David hops up from our table to get another serving of pasta for his two girls, who sit on either side of their mom. Though I'm only half-Jewish, I did have my bat mitzvah at a Reform synagogue. I also went to Israel when I was sixteen. (When I was there, a Hasidic rabbi explained to our youth group who was a Jew in his book, and who wasn't—meaning *me*, the girl with the Catholic mother. I was crushed.)

"Mommy, you turned Jewish when I came out of you," is how Mae puts it. In a way, she's right. No, I didn't give her a Jewish name or have a baby-naming ceremony. But when we moved to California, I enrolled her in the local Jewish preschool. I've been struck by how warm and close-knit this community is. Mothers are always inviting classmates to their homes to play and posting sign-up sheets to help families in need. Wasn't it this compassion that has always drawn me to Judaism? I feel grateful to the caring cluster of local Jews who've embraced my daughter and me.

Mae has learned how to belt out Shabbat songs, recite the menu of any Jewish holiday feast, and tell the Passover story of

King Pharaoh, how Moses led the Israelites to freedom when the Red Sea parted. "But Mommy, the Red Sea isn't really red, is it?" she always asks as she recites the story. She's proud of her Jewish identity.

I write a monthly column about the Jewish dating scene in the Bay Area in *J.,* a local Jewish newspaper. What Jewish dating scene? I'm not in New York anymore. *Duh.*

Why aren't men like Warren or Josh approaching me?

Because they're already married.

But now there's Adam. I think I've met my hot, manly Jewish man.

When we arrive at the JCC at 6 PM the next night, Adam has saved us seats in the front row right next to him.

Damn, he's hot with a capital "H." I want to close my eyes and rub my hand over his smooth head.

The play, *The Sad Kingdom,* begins, and I hold Mae on my lap. I'm so nervous that I hug her too tightly.

"Stop squeezing me, Mommy!" she says.

"Sorry, honey."

When I turn my head, I catch a glimpse of Adam's bicep. This guy works out.

He leans over and whispers in my ear, "I'm dying to know what your story is."

I shudder. "I'm curious to know yours, too," I whisper back.

"It's pretty short and simple," he says.

"So is mine," I say.

After the play, he takes us—his two girls, my girl, and me—out for frozen yogurt. We all get toppings. As the girls sit on the bench, gulping down their treats, we tell our stories in whispery voices, about our exes splitting town and managing on our own as single parents.

Adam and I never really go out on a real date after getting together for the play. After all, we're both single parents who get no help from the other parent—so how much dating can we do? I hear a lot of gossip among Jewish women around Berkeley: that he's certainly one good-looking hunk of a man and has gone out with a lot of women around town.

The next couple of months we eat dinner together every week at his place: Adam, his two girls, Mae, and me. Adam is a fine cook, a loving father, and a great disciplinarian (what else would you expect from a police officer?). I pick up a lot of parenting tips from him.

After dinner, we often go into the hot tub together in his back yard or watch a video. At Adam's one night, Mae watches *Willy Wonka & the Chocolate Factory* for the first time, and it remains one of her all-time favorite movies.

His daughters are biracial, too, supersweet and intelligent girls who take Mae under their wing. When we pick up Adam and his girls at the airport after their weekend trip to Disneyland, they have a Minnie Mouse toothbrush for Mae. She uses it right away, in the car.

Adam's passion is writing music, and one night, in his recording studio, he sings and records a lullaby for Mae so she can listen to it on the way home to fall asleep.

Everything seems perfect. But something is missing. I can't put my finger on it exactly. We are friends. We are companions. Yet nothing more. There's simply no emotional connection.

We share one long kiss, and that's it. Maybe it's that he's a cop and I'm a reporter. Or that he drives an SUV and I drive a hybrid-electric. Or that our emotional bond is blank. There is simply no feeling. That's not a good recipe for love.

Still, Adam has given me a taste of Jewish men. I'm ready to savor more.

Chapter Eight:
JDate, Here I Come

Summer 2005, I decide to give online dating another chance—this time, with a Jewish twist. I've been rediscovering my Jewish roots, and logging on to JDate seems like a good way to intermingle my renewed Jewish identity with dating. Maybe a shared cultural background is just my ticket to true love?

After all, I write a monthly column on dating for *J.* And I've recently started facilitating my own weekly singles group at the Berkeley-Richmond Jewish Community Center, for singles who want to get back on the dating scene after a breakup.

I vow to be an advocate for singles, as they learn about themselves and the life partner they wish for. I advertise my seminar as a "no-nonsense, interactive group that makes dating fun, safe, and successful." Surely, I know plenty of strategies by now for meeting and screening potential life partners. And red flags? Don't get me started. Every week, I give out homework, asking questions such as, "What are your values?" and "Are you clear about your deal breakers?"

I log on to JDate, thinking a nice, hot, manly Jewish man would be just the ticket. The first thing I do is read the "Mazel Tov" section, scrolling through the hundreds of couples who met here and got married. Could that be me one day? I'm skeptical.

Still, I post an ad: "I am a warm and generous single mom who is looking for a wholesome man. . . . What I enjoy: a good book, fresh berries, Lake Anza, and holding hands. I've put a lot of energy into exploring myself—have you?"

Of course, when I show my profile to my friends, Siobhan calls me on it.

"You've put a lot of energy into exploring yourself?" she says. "Do you mean to imply what I think you do?"

"What?" I say, clueless.

"Exploring yourself, Rachel, could also imply masturbation."

I hadn't quite thought about it that way. As usual, her judgment rules the day. I nix the sentence.

I've come a long way since I first put myself online in 2003. Back then, on Match.com, I was a newbie, unsure of what I wanted and, in hindsight, not nearly solid enough in my independence to get into a relationship. Two years later, at almost thirty-three, I know what matters: my clan of friends, my writing, my organic fruits and veggies, my bedtime stories with my daughter.

The last line of my online profile reads, "My daughter means the world to me—and more."

I have a stronger hold on single motherhood now. I make my living as a writer. I cook a mean veggie stir-fry. I pay the rent on time. I set limits with my daughter. Where's that vulnerable woman who couldn't even mutter the words, "I'm a single mom" on a date? She's long gone.

Three months earlier, I file the paperwork at the Alameda County Courthouse for sole custody. I also file for child support, which I know I'll never see, but it is good to let the tears fall over my calculations of diapers, groceries, rent, and preschool. The numbers prove that Eric has missed every point in Mae's life: her first steps, her first song, her first "I love you," her hair done up in little braids, her first time writing her own name. I submit page upon page to the judge about when Eric left us, the attempts I made to get support, the futility of it all.

When he pounds his gavel in the courtroom—"Sole and physical custody granted"—his voice resonates through me. And for the first time I truly feel that Eric and I will never be together again.

Now I'm going on a blind date with a man who says his ideal relationship is "two complete human beings who jump the hurdles of life together." I'm ready to jump, but I know the best thing for me is to take it one step at a time.

This turns out to be harder than it sounds. Just setting up our first date makes me feel like I'm walking in place. "I work until eight every night in the city," he tells me during our first conversation. "I'm available after that."

"You can't meet me until eight thirty?" I ask.

"Or nine," he says.

"That's kind of late for me," I say.

"Weekends work best for me," he says.

"So, let's say this works out, and I want to see you on a weeknight?" I say.

"Impossible. But we could still talk on the phone during the week."

I haven't even met this guy and we're having our first spat. But what's amazing is how, after a few years of dating, I can spot a red flag waving a half mile away. I don't always want to see it, but it's there nonetheless. His flag reads in big, bold letters: I'M UNAVAILABLE.

Now that I'm savvier, I can see it all clearly. So, why don't I call it off right now? Because I haven't even met him. Because I can't help but wonder if I'm being too critical. Because it's my pattern to see a red flag and keep on going. I always root for the underdog even if I know from the get-go that he's not going to win. But he has one more thing to tell me.

"It's my birthday on Friday," he says.

"It is? That's great! But you must have other plans."

"No," he says.

"Aren't you doing something with friends?"

"No."

There goes the other red flag, waving along with the first one. Is this guy a loner? A workaholic without friends? Still, I feel for him. Birthdays mean the world to me. I couldn't care less about Christmas. But a birthday is always special.

"Well, is there something you want to do to celebrate?" I ask him.

"It will just be great to meet you," he says. "But no pressure. Really."

No pressure. As if a blind date isn't pressure enough. Life as a single mom has enough pressure as it is, with all the demands on my time and energy: Mae's hair and teeth brushed, school lunch made, underwear clean, permission slip filled out. Then it's my turn. Add to this the pressure of finding childcare, taking a shower, ironing my clothes, getting dressed, putting on lipstick. That's enough to make a woman lose it. And that's before I even go out on my date.

I meet Guy for our first date at Cesar's, a trendy bar in North Berkeley. I know the Gourmet Ghetto on Shattuck Avenue well by now, having lived in Berkeley for three years. Guy is a forty-four-year-old human resources consultant who has never married. He lives with his dog. His username on JDate is "Shining Armor." He's looking for a woman who truly wants to love and be loved, he says.

I'm a sucker for a good writer, and Guy is no exception. "I believe in love at first sight, yet I am grounded enough to pay my bills on time," his profile reads. "Are you able to let go of your grasp on the past and get lost in love?"

You bet I am.

Guy tells me I'll recognize him because he looks just like his picture. I think that's odd; he has only one photo on JDate, and it's blurry. I can barely make him out. Red-flag alert. Still, somehow in my overactive imagination, I've turned him into a tall, dark, and captivating prince. (Don't ask me where I got the "tall" part, since his stats clearly state that he is only five foot seven.)

So what do you get for a man on his birthday when you've never met him before? Good question. When I ask one of my good friends, who tends to be right about these kinds of things, she says to get a chocolate raspberry cupcake and a candle. You know—cute, sweet, but not too forward.

I also jot down a note on a three-by-five card: "Happy Birthday Guy! I'm honored to be on a blind date with you on your birthday. This is certainly a first for me. —Rachel"

When I call Siobhan to tell her my birthday–blind date plan, she says, "I wish I could be taken out on a date with you!"

When I arrive at the bar, a short, chunky man is standing in the front. Sure, he has short brown hair and brown eyes like his photo, but his cheeks are fat. And his pants are too long.

"Rachel!" he says, offering me his hand.

I shake it heartily. I mean business. But he takes mine like a wet washcloth. Not a good sign.

When he turns around to open the door for me, there's something flaking off the back of his scalp near his neck. Dandruff? Sunburn?

The bar is packed; there isn't an empty table. I tell Guy that I'm fine standing. What I don't tell him is, "I could really use a drink right now."

"We're not going to wait," he tells the hostess.

He says this without checking with me first. Oh man, this is going to be a long night.

We walk across the street, to a Mexican restaurant, and order appetizers. He doesn't like salsa. We talk about his job helping people write their résumés and my recent gig writing a history book for middle school students. He hasn't asked me one question about Mae. Not one. If a man doesn't acknowledge that she's my core, there's no future.

Still, talking is effortless; he could be my long-lost cousin. There's no heat, but there's comfort. Chemistry is a funny thing; my knees do not buzz, my heart doesn't skip. He's a nice guy, like plenty of the nice guys I've met during the last few years of dating. Nice. But I want more than nice.

A few nights later, Mae is lying on the living room rug drawing in her sketchbook. At age five, she's a master artist, levels above where I'll ever be. She loves to draw self-portraits, with her puffy pigtails and light brown freckles. I turn on the computer. Three new emails are waiting from men on JDate. I'm glued to the screen. But all of a sudden, Mae is right next to me.

"Mommy, is that *you?*" She's pointing to my headshot on the screen. It's a little black-and-white photo that Siobhan took of me this summer.

"Yes."

"But it doesn't look like you."

"It doesn't?" Maybe she's right; my smile looks forced. Am I too posed?

"Why is your picture up there?"

Over the next few weeks, I line up a few more dates.

Forty-five-year-old Jay is "a culturally literate, athletic, passionate, giving never-married man" and an environmental lawyer. On the phone, I can't get past his annoying voice. At the end of our first conversation, he says, "Ciao, Bella." We never actually make it out for a date.

Amid intrigues me because he gave his sperm to a couple of lesbian friends last year—something he tells me right off the bat. I'm all in favor, but telling me as part of a getting-to-know-you phone chat? While this is not a red flag, it's not exactly green either. He sees his little girl, his one-year-old daughter, on weekends. Amid wants to know what I mean when I say that I'm looking for a "wholesome man."

Good question. Maybe I should have said "healthy" or "decent." Or maybe just "a good man." But I like the way that "wholesome" sounds. And besides, I'd describe myself as wholesome.

"Do I have to be completely wholesome?" he asks.

"Yes," I say, teasing. "One hundred percent."

"Then define wholesome," he says.

"Sincere, genuine, trustworthy," I say. "No, I'm not looking for a farmer from the cornfields."

But when we meet for an early pasta dinner, I can't get over his huge potbelly. Yuck. Not exactly appetizing.

One night, "Toby1972" sends me an instant message asking if I'd like to chat.

Whenever a man offers to IM, I hesitate.

Part of the excitement about meeting men online is being able to draft witty notes, to take my time as I ponder over what to say. IM is so, well, instant. I'm afraid it will speed things up way too fast for me. When you're trying to read and type at the same time, it's hard to grasp someone's tone. Is he being sarcastic? IM is too flirty too fast.

Moreover, I've never been good at computer lingo:

CID *Consider it done*
TTYL *Talk to you later*
YT? *You there?*

Then I click on Toby's profile. Yes, I want to IM. He's a very cute thirty-three-year-old stockbroker originally from Boston with sandy blond hair and blue eyes. He has gold-rimmed glasses. He's half Israeli. He's left-handed. He describes himself as "spontaneous, easygoing, and responsible."

He wants to be with a woman he can "fold with." *Sure, I'll fold with you.*

"I decided to give JDate a try just this weekend after much thought," he says. "So, you're new here, too?"

"Yes," I say. "And you're my very first IM."

"How lucky I am," he says. "You have beautiful hair."

"Thanks. You have lovely glasses."

"How old is your daughter?" he asks. (Note: Big score for Toby!)

"Five," I write.

And all of a sudden, there's a pause. I'm staring at the blank screen, waiting. I hold my fingers over the keys. Nothing. Was it something I said?

"I hate IM," he finally writes. "Want to chat on the phone? Old-school style?"

"Chat on the phone right now?" I say. "We just got started here! Goodness, you are fast."

"No, don't take it that way," he says.

"I don't even know what your favorite food is," I tease.

"Lasagna," he says. "But really, there's no rush."

I ask him to send me his phone number. I go offline and take another quick look at his profile. I'm caught off guard. He writes, "I am open to any kind of woman. I don't have any specific requirements."

How can you be out there dating and *not* have any specific requirements? My requirements could fill an entire page! I want to have an open, honest, and passionate relationship with a man who communicates well, and whose love will abound for my daughter and me. He is financially responsible and full of laughter. A tall order, but at least I know what I want—finally.

Is this guy flaky, or what?

At this point, I'm clear about what I want. No, it's *not* a checklist of the top one hundred qualities a man must have. But I have a clear vision of my future relationship. I know what my standards are.

Still, as usual I don't follow my gut and instead call Toby. We talk for an hour, laughing about how absurd online dating can be. Both of us were born in 1972. We've both been to Prague. We both love anything curried.

On Sunday morning, Toby is waiting for me at a local coffee shop. We reach out and hug, spontaneous and easy. He invites me to come to a yoga class with him sometime, the Berkeley equivalent of a movie. Not only is he nice, he sparkles. He's also financially stable. He makes me laugh. After our date, he's off to New York for a week on a business trip.

We exchange email messages. "It was great to meet you."

"You too. I enjoyed your company."

"Want to meet again when I get back?"

"Sure!"

He calls me the night he gets back.

"Want to go to IKEA with me on Friday?" he asks.

"I'd love to!" I say. "We can share Swedish meatballs."

He wants to get some things for his apartment. At IKEA. It's definitely metrosexual; I have to say I can see the glimmer of a red flag out of the corner of my eye.

My stepdad offers to take Mae overnight so I'll have the whole night ahead of me. On Friday, the traffic to my stepdad's in Walnut Creek is horrendous. I'm talking to myself at the wheel: *This is all worth it. I like this guy.*

"I don't have a daddy," Mae suddenly says from the back seat.

"What, honey?" I ask, thinking I misheard her.

"I don't have a daddy," she says again.

I've been waiting for years for this. Well, not exactly like *this*. I thought she'd put it in a question, as in, "Mommy, do I have a daddy?"

Instead, she's so matter-of-fact; she could be talking about the weather. *I don't have a daddy. The sky is gray today.*

I have a collage of baby pictures on our living room wall, one of which is a little picture of Mae with her father, Eric. We'd gone to New Jersey to visit some friends, and he's sitting with three-month-old Mae on their sofa. He stares ahead blankly, looking troubled. The last time Mae and I looked at the photos on our wall, about six months ago, I told her, "This is your father. He helped bring you into the world and—"

She leapt up, leaving my sentence hanging.

"Let's play Chutes and Ladders!" she said. Evidently, it was not the time to talk about it.

It's not like this is the first time she's brought up a daddy-missing-in-action. When we first moved to Berkeley, Mae and I made our very first male friend right around the corner. We were on an afternoon walk, and Hunter was bent over a well-known "art car," gluing plastic fruit to its side. Mae was immediately drawn to him (and the car). As time passed, Hunter and I developed a deep platonic friendship. Nowadays, he often drops by our apartment with books and clothes for Mae.

One afternoon just before Mae's fourth birthday, Hunter walked to the local park with us. Mae wanted him to push her on the swing. Just as Hunter pulled the swing back, ready to let go, Mae turned her head.

"Are you my daddy?" she asked.

Hunter gripped the swing tighter. "I'm kind of like your daddy, because I care about you," he answered. "I guess you could call me your godfather."

"What's God?" Mae asked.

Hunter laughed, knowing that he was in for it.

Now, on the way to Walnut Creek, maybe it's time to talk about Dad. Truthfully.

"Do your friends at school ask if you have a daddy?" I ask her.

"Yes," she says.

I peer into the rearview mirror to look at her. I'm holding my breath, waiting for her to ask me more. Like, "Who is my daddy?"

"What do you say when your friends ask if you have a daddy?" I ask.

"I just say that I don't have one," she says, straightforward and cheerful. She seems so confident with her single-mama family. But I know this can't be her answer forever.

■▩▨▩ ▨

After dropping Mae off with my stepfather, I'm back in the car. It took us an hour in heavy traffic to get here. Now I'll spend another hour trying to get through the Caldecott Tunnel on my way to IKEA near Berkeley.

My cell phone is buzzing.

It's Toby. "Hi, Rachel."

"Hi! I just made it through the tunnel," I say. "I'm almost there!"

"Look," he says. "I feel really horrible about this, but I have to cancel for tonight."

"What's wrong?"

"Nothing's wrong, exactly. I had a work meeting with some investors, and I accidentally wrote it down for next Friday. It's really tonight. There's no way I can get out of it."

"Oh," I say, as I slump over the steering wheel. I'm not breathing.

"I'll make it up to you," he says.

Make it up to me? Sure buddy, go ahead and make it up to me. I want to scream, *Do you have any idea what I had to go through to get childcare tonight? Don't you investors carry around Palm Pilots? What's wrong with you?*

But really, I'm just disappointed. I liked him.

A few days later, he leaves me a message saying that he'll be out of town for a week on business. Two weeks later, he calls back to say hi. I never follow up.

I have a game plan. With my *J.* column, I can look for my soul mate, who I'm convinced is Jewish, and actually get paid to do it. A Jewish Carrie Bradshaw—with a kid. Siobhan and Arden cheer me on.

"You go girl!" Siobhan says. But ever-cautious, she adds, "I sure wouldn't put myself out there like that. Please be careful."

Three years ago, when I became a stringer for *J.,* my aim wasn't about reconnecting with my Jewish roots. This was strictly professional. I'd sent my resume to various publications when I got to California, and *J.* was one of many to take me on. All of this happened by accident.

My first column for *J.* is about sending Mae to a Jewish summer camp for the first time. I vaguely hint that I am a single parent. But, *bam,* in my second column, I lay out the facts: "I'm a 33-year-old single mom seeking a man who avoids drama and braids challah. . . . I insist that the man in our lives is drama- and drug-free, open and honest, responsible and very fond of children. . . . My daughter will be firm that the man in our lives can hide matzah and sing 'Zum Gali Gali'"—a traditional Jewish campfire song.

Zum gali gali gali, zum gali gali
Zum gali gali gali, zum gali gali
Let us work, my friends as one
Let us work 'til the task is done
Let us work, my friends as one
Let us work 'til the task is done

There's a problem, however. Remember that Hasidic rabbi who didn't consider me a real Jew? Turns out he's not the only one. I find out that some Jewish guys see me as a fraud because I was raised by an Irish Catholic mother and a Jewish father.

Reform Judaism, in which I was raised, considers a person to be Jewish if either of the parents are Jewish and the child is raised Jewish. I had my bat mitzvah. I went to Jewish camps every summer for a decade. But because my mom is *not* Jewish, many Jewish men don't consider me to be a true Jew. It stops plenty of men in their tracks—and *not* because they want to date me. Harsh letters land in my in-box:

If you and I were across a table in a café I would have more loyalty to Judaism and the Jewish people than to a woman I just met, no matter how bright, beautiful, and sexy she might be.

Reform Judaism is basically a fraud. Why don't you just undergo an Orthodox conversion?

Uh-oh. What have I gotten myself into here? As more critical emails arrive, I start to get insecure. What if I'm *not* Jewish enough? Then again, what if they're full of shit?

Sure it's important to share a common background and interests, or at least it's helpful. But what about those things you can't put a label on—the ability to be kind and respectful and true? To be a good listener and have a balanced attitude toward life?

I wonder if I'm really up for being judged like this.

I haven't stepped into a synagogue for over a decade.

My daughter doesn't go to Hebrew school.

I can't recognize even one Hebrew letter anymore.

We don't celebrate Shabbat regularly.

I don't have a mezuzah on my door. I don't even know how to spell that word.

What if the Jewish man I'm looking for insists on turning off the TV every Friday and lighting the Sabbath candles?

What if my daughter doesn't want to have a bat mitzvah when she's thirteen?

Am I really up for this?

Hmmm, maybe not.

But mixed in with the vindictive mail are plenty of nice messages from Jewish men who *do* seem to accept me for who I am:

I liked your column. Any interest in meeting a single Jewish father?

I love kids and have been to Israel several times. I'd like to meet a nice, sweet woman like you.

I'm a romantic and handsome surgeon who seeks a woman of exquisite beauty. If this resonates, let's exchange images.

Maybe this wasn't such a bad idea.

But this letter really makes me pause:

I too am single and find myself bemoaning the difficulty of meeting single Jewish women. So, I'm writing to you. I could tell you many things about me, but for now, I'll include a description from a female friend: "Tall, athletic, good-looking with extraordinary wit. Has a huge heart and a good soul, owns his own washing machine (and home) and loves kids. Must learn to give himself a break once in a while. Don't let this one get away."

I fall in love with him on the computer screen. I'm hopeful and enthusiastic. *Please, Mr. Life Partner, be there for me. I'm ready for you.*

But tonight, as I sit across from the author of the above email, I'm having doubts. He's my third Jewish man in two weeks, a never-married mortgage broker—maybe I've reached my quota.

I've already been out with a forty-six-year-old, balding psychologist who analyzed me over dinner. "There's so much sadness in you," he told me. I also met the forty-one-year-old divorced father of a teenager who still fights with his ex-wife regularly. Not exactly what I had hoped for.

My rabbi during childhood, whom I haven't spoken to in fifteen years, comes across one of my columns and emails me. Even he tries to set me up with a friend of his. Again, stimulating conversation, but no glimmers of passion.

Don't get me wrong. Every Jewish man I've gone out with so far has been nice. And thoughtful. And considerate. But not *the one.*

What's wrong with this picture? Siobhan tells me that I've got to look at "the cross section" of a man.

"It seems investment bankers hot to trot on JDate aren't gonna zest your nipple," she tells me in an email. "Somewhere, there are some hot kabbalah-spinning, Cajun-chicken-bakin', hot lovers—who will also respect and adore you . . . and preferably not be too broke."

Doug is tall and slender, and dressed conservatively in a tweed jacket and ironed khaki pants. His face is emotionless. I can't tell if he's always this cool, or if he simply doesn't like me. Not a good sign.

My knees are crossed under my tight turquoise sequined skirt—yes, my first-date skirt once again. I'm tired of this skirt. I'm tired of all these first dates. No wonder this skirt is looking so worn. I wish I could give it a break. Maybe *I* need a break.

I should be focused on the man across the table. But my mind is elsewhere. I'm thinking about the fact that the milk carton in our refrigerator is almost empty. Will there be enough for Mae's oatmeal in the morning? Did I forget to turn on the washing machine? I hope she has some clean underwear for tomorrow. Damn, I forgot to check her school's lost-and-found for her missing jacket.

Right now, I should be laughing merrily, but I'm wondering whether my daughter is eating dinner. I imagine her eating two small bites of pasta before jumping up from the table to play with her friend. When I pick her up, I wonder if she'll say (as she often does), "Mommy, I'm hungry!"

Besides, Doug is not quite as good-looking as I'd hoped. He has tired, deep lines under his eyes, and he seems self-conscious. When I'd asked by email how old he was, he didn't want to say.

When I ask him again now—"So, how old are you?"—he shakes his head. I feel irritated.

He laughs, but he still won't tell me. "Guess," he says.

But I don't want to play this game on a Tuesday night. I want to get out of here. I want to drive away in my car and pick up my daughter. I want to hear all about her day at school. Still, I'm drinking chardonnay and eating sautéed eggplant. Fine, I'll do this, even though it's painful and I'd rather be curled up on the couch with my daughter watching *Toy Story.*

"Early forties?" I ask.

No, he's forty-eight, fifteen years older than I am. I smile. I like mature men. I definitely deserve one. Just *not* one who could practically be my father.

But he doesn't seem very comfortable with the number. And frankly neither do I. "That's quite a gap," he says.

I take the final sip of my wine, and for a split second, I slip away into a carefree void. I almost forget that it's dark outside. I almost disregard the fact that it's bedtime for my five-year-old.

"Do you know what time it is?" I ask casually.

Doug looks down at his watch: "Seven thirty."

"Oh!" I gasp. "It's a school night!"

"You need to go?"

"Yes."

Outside, he and I give each other a quick embrace. I'm sure he wouldn't "zest my nipple," as Siobhan would say. During the drive back, I feel guilty. What a waste of time. I could have eaten dinner with my daughter and heard all about which kids she played with today and which book her reading buddy shared with her. I could have relaxed at home with her, instead of scrambling to find childcare. When I pick her up now, she'll be exhausted, like me.

By the time I reach Siobhan's house, the mom in me is back. I hug Mae and we head home, where she goes straight to the bathroom. "I have to poop, Mom," she tells me.

After we get ready for bed, I snuggle up next to her and read a story. I close my eyes, and breathe, catching a whiff of Doug on my forearm. His cologne must have rubbed off on me when we hugged. I won't be smelling him again anytime soon. I'm just glad to be home with my daughter. As I hold Mae close, I can't help but wonder if, one evening, the scent of a man I love dearly will rub off on me. When that happens, I'll breathe him in deeply.

It is fall 2005, and Mae is starting kindergarten. My baby is a girl now.

She wants to know about mammals versus egg-laying animals, asking, "Mom, do baby whales come out of eggs?" And then, "Why not?"

She stands on a step stool and helps me cut vegetables before dinner—with a plastic knife. She can count by tens. She helps out around the house, if persuaded: She puts her dirty clothes in the hamper, gets snacks out of the refrigerator, and brushes her teeth. We have pedicure parties in the bathroom. We even share jewelry.

When Hazel, Siobhan's five-year-old daughter, comes over for the afternoon, I eavesdrop by the bedroom door as they play with dolls.

"This one is the daddy," says Hazel, holding up a boy-doll.

"Let's pretend there's no daddy, okay?" Mae says.

"Okay," Hazel agrees, putting the boy-doll back in the bin.

I hold my breath in the doorway, feeling proud of Mae— and proud of the family I've created with my girlfriends, Mae's friends at school, my dad, and my sister. I've created a family for Mae, man or not.

One afternoon, Mae has a friend over after summer camp. I'm stirring a pot of pasta on the stove when I hear her friend say, "Do you have a daddy?"

My fingers tightly squeeze the wooden spoon. Should I rush over and explain? How will Mae handle this question on her own?

"I have a birth father," Mae says. "His name is Eric."

A birth father. You go, Mae. Berkeley has been good for this girl.

"Then where is he?" this friend wants to know.

"He lives far away," Mae says.

End of conversation. They're off to play dress-up.

On her first day of kindergarten, Mae is wearing a pink, flowery polyester dress my mom gave her. We park in front of the school, and I hop out of the car with my digital camera.

"Cheese!" Mae says.

Just when I press the button, she jumps right in front of the camera, up close.

"Please, just one picture," I beg.

"Of my eyeball!" she says, putting her eye close to the lens.

She's such a goofball. With a quick kiss and a "Bye, Mom!" she's off.

During the walk back to the car, I hold it together, alone among all these kindergarten couple-parents. Back in my car, however, I slump over the steering wheel and bawl my head off. It's one of those hard cries, the kind when you're crying so hard that you're shuddering like when you were a kid. The windows are steamed up. I have to catch my breath.

When I calm down, I call everyone to tell them the big news—my baby is now in kindergarten. My mom and stepdad. My dad. Siobhan and Arden. Our neighbor, Hunter. I'm so proud of Mae—of the calm and happy kid she has become.

Despite all the dates, all the years of deconstructing ads on Match.com and JDate, all the boring blind dates I've been on—and all the years of misery thinking that Eric and I could patch things up—Mae and her happiness are what really matter.

After only a few weeks of kindergarten, one of the moms in Mae's class tells me that she calls my daughter "the Zen girl" because she's so poised and mellow. Another mom tells me that Mae has a calm about her that is far beyond her years. I can't help but smile. At school, yes, she is composed. But a daily drama often takes place in our girl house, going from comedy to tragedy within minutes. This morning, she doesn't like the way I've brushed her pigtails. This evening, I ask her six times to *please* pick up her dirty socks off the floor. Both of us are sensitive and moody. But we've always been that way, come to think of it.

Still, most of the time, Mae is being the Zen kindergartner, while I remain the dramatic mom looking for a man who can join our entertaining lives.

In addition to getting the standard email responses to my column in *J.*—"My name is Mark, and I love your column . . . I'm attaching a photo. . . . You'll probably get snowed with all kinds of email from eligible guys, but maybe you'll consider one on the Peninsula?"—one day I find the following:

I have a friend who sounds like a lot of what you are looking for. He's a 38-year-old actor and musician in San Francisco, a wonderful guy and an old friend of mine. I'd be glad to give you more info.

That's one thing about the Jewish community—they're the original matchmakers.

I'm swamped with emails from twenty different Jewish men right now: What have I done? Is it too late to back out? I'm tired. I can't keep up. But I tell myself it's all in a day's work.

By the time I finally start to draft a note to Aaron, the actor and musician, he has already written to me:

I figured I'd just jump in here! My life is simple; I have my job, my art, and my friends. I love dinners and movies with friends— and playing in a street hockey league—though my ankles, knees and back aren't too happy about it—performing improvisation, and playing music.

Aaron attaches a professional acting photo of himself to the email, and damn, this guy is cute. He has an adorable, boyish face, sandy brown hair, and silver-rimmed glasses. I'm so psyched to get a note from a cutie like this that I immediately forward the email and photo to Arden at work.

I write, "A local doctor who read my column just passed his childhood friend on to me by email. How sweet. Check him out! Thoughts? Love, Rachel."

She writes back right away: "Sooooo . . . funny!! I know Aaron very well. What a *coinky-dinc.* We didn't actually date, but we did kiss. Still, there would be nothing weird to me about you going out with him. He's very funny, political, and has a great body. He's very busy, though. I think you should go out with him."

Boy, the Bay Area Jewish community is close-knit: They all seem to know each other, much more so than in New York. The fact that Arden knows Aaron reassures me, like he's been prescreened.

Aaron and I meet for coffee after I drop Mae off at kindergarten. We talk about his most recent play—he's got the lead role—and my newspaper column. We talk about the kind of music we listen to and how tough it can be living in the Bay Area. But time and time again, our conversation circles back to Arden.

"What's she up to?" he asks, and I fill him in about her job and daughter. I could talk about Arden for hours. I adore her.

"Is she seeing anyone?" he wants to know.

"Uh . . ."

"What I always loved about Arden is that she made me laugh," he says. And when he says it, he has this forlorn yet promising look in his eyes. *Ah, Arden. He misses Arden.*

After a brief hug outside the coffee shop, I call Arden right away on my cell, and say, "He still likes you!"

"No, he doesn't," she says.

"Yes, he does!"

I feel like I'm back in junior high. Maybe in the end, it is better that he wasn't right for either of us. Besides now Arden has a boyfriend, and she's pumped up to do some matchmaking for me. She tells me that she wants to introduce me to a Jewish real estate agent she once dated.

"He'll make a good column," she teases.

"That's awful!" I say. "I'm not going on a date unless he's worth it."

"There was no chemistry between us," she says. "But you never know. He writes, too."

A writer? Well, that's a possibility. I'll take a chance on a writer any day.

My mom, who's visiting this fall from Morocco, arrives ten minutes before my date. I tell her, "You can say your hellos from the top of the stairs, but you cannot come to the door."

"Yes, ma'am!" she says, and heads off to find Mae.

It's enough that my daughter will be meeting my date tonight. But c'mon now, I'm thirty-three. The idea of my mom meeting him, too, seems absurd.

Mae is in the kitchen, making Jewish stars at her art table, and I give her the drill: "No sugar snacks, teeth brushed . . ."

"You look pretty, Mommy," Mae says, ignoring my litany.

"So, how do you know Stan?" my mom asks.

"He's recycled," I say.

My mom raises her eyebrows.

"Arden and I are being environmentally conscious," I say, teasing her. "We pass men around after we're done with them."

My mom bites her lower lip.

"C'mon, mom!" I laugh. "He's Jewish, forty-five years old, never married," I say, pretending like Mae is not catching every word, when I know this is really inappropriate.

Stan recently relocated to the Bay Area from Baltimore. He also has an MFA in creative writing.

The doorbell rings.

"There he is!" my mom says excitedly.

I smooth out my sarong and descend the stairs. When I open the door, both my mom and Mae are at the top of the staircase.

"Hello there!" my mom says in her flirtatious, singsong voice.

"Hello there!" Mae mimics.

When I look at Stan in his jeans and a white, collared, button-down shirt, I feel overdressed in my flowing cotton skirt and high-heeled sandals. Still, something about his casualness looks comfortably informal—I can imagine him cheering from the sidelines of a kids' soccer match.

I block his body, not letting him inside. "I'm glad everyone had the chance to meet!" I say, and slam the door behind me.

As we get into his car, Stan says, "Wow, I can't remember the last time I met a woman's mother on a date."

"Yeah, and I even have a ten o'clock curfew," I say, trying to make light of the situation. But the truth is, as I sink down in the seat, I feel very small.

What are you doing with your life? I think. *You still have boys knocking at the door to meet your mom!* Not only that, but my kid was right there, greeting him. That's a lot for a man to handle on a first date.

But none of this is the real reason why I shut the door so fast behind us: Really, I want first right of refusal. It matters immensely how my mom and daughter feel about the man who's taking me out. However, I get to look and see first, and then decide whether he gets to come upstairs to meet my family. When I invite a man inside my house to meet my daughter, it's quite an honor: It means letting him enter my most personal space.

Stan is telling me about his synagogue, but I'm lost in my own thoughts. *What if I had invited him in, and introduced him to my family, the old-fashioned way? Isn't that what happens in traditional Jewish families? Don't you introduce a suitor to your mom? Maybe when I was sixteen. Snap out of it, Rachel.*

But I do like the tradition of introducing a man to those who are closest to me. I imagine what would have unfolded had I invited Stan upstairs. My mother would have asked him where he went to college and what he does for a living. Then Mae would have rushed in with her drawing and thrust it into his lap. Would he have glanced at it quickly and said, "Nice!" Or, would he have held the picture, examined it carefully, and asked, "Can you tell me about what you've drawn here?"

When a man meets my child, it's a true test. Will he bend down on one knee and talk to her face to face? Or will he ignore her as she hovers at his legs, and look into my eyes instead?

Over dinner, Stan and I talk about our parents and our Jewish education. I wait for him to ask about my daughter, but he doesn't. His potential as father material is not looking good, and I'm anxious about how the night will end.

When he parks the car in front of my house, he leans over for a goodnight kiss, but I'm grateful for my old-fashioned excuse to turn my cheek and jump out of the car.

When I get back home, I'm tired. My mom gives me a kiss and heads home. When I go into Mae's room to check on her, I lean my head on her bedpost.

I wish I could tell my mom how disappointed I am with the string of dates I've had over the past year. But my mom and I don't really talk. I don't know if we ever have. I used to love to hear about her whirlwind courtship in San Francisco in 1969 with my father. My mom was a waitress at the Stagecoach Inn where my dad had lunch every day; my parents fell madly in love and got married three months later.

They had two kids in three years. I was born in the summer of 1972, with the help of forceps. Seventeen months later, my sister, Rebecca, shot out like a rocket. But my free-spirited, sometimes-depressed mother had always wanted to be a poet and wasn't satisfied in her marriage. They got divorced when I was three. Growing up, my sister and I spent three days a week with Dad and four days with Mom.

Just after Mae was born, my then-fifty-three-year-old mom was awarded a Fulbright in Morocco. Just like that, she packed her bags and left the suburbs of Northern California to move to Rabat. My stepfather stayed here. So did I. The truth, as we all know, is often layered and complicated. I've never completely forgiven her for coming and going these past six years. Every year, I find myself wishing that she'd be here Mae's birthday. But she never is.

It's not really the man I'm disappointed with tonight.

It's my mom.

It's a lifelong disappointment that I feel, and the only way I can forgive her is by becoming what was missing in my own life: the mom I wish I'd had.

Chapter Nine: Matchmaker, Matchmaker

"Matchmaker, Matchmaker," reads the subject line of the email that arrives in the early Fall of 2005.

"I have an amazing Jewish man for you to meet," the writer begins. "He's not my son, nor my grandson, nor my brother. He's my husband's best friend."

Over the past four years, I've gone on Match.com dates, blind dates, and disaster dates. Who *is* this woman? Her name is Dianna, and she signs her name, "The Yenta," which means a woman who gossips and meddles in others' affairs. The Yenta goes on to tell me about her husband's friend: "He's from Israel, in his early forties, and has lived in the Bay Area for almost two decades. He has many friends, a great job, a home . . . but what's missing is a family."

What's missing is a family? Well, that pretty much describes Mae and me.

One of Judaism's highest good deeds is matchmaking. But I'm still floored: This kind stranger has taken the time and energy to write me a long note about this man who "adores kids" and is always looking "longingly at families."

What man does that? *Um, none that I know.*

"I wouldn't actually call him 'nice,'" she adds. "He's Israeli, and he has that tough kibbutznik exterior."

Uh-oh. He's not nice. What's that supposed to mean? When I read on, however, that bit about Mr.-Not-Nice falls by the wayside. "He really is the sweetest guy with the biggest heart. He's also funny, sexy, kind, generous, and just rock-solid. I know for sure that whoever he ends up with will be blessed, adored, and cared for."

She adds that I can contact her for more information. C'mon now, what more do I need? What kind of woman would *not* want to meet this man?

I write back and ask her if this guy knows what she's up to.

"He gave me permission to write to you," she says. "But he had no idea *what* I would write. Tonight, I read him my email, which I thought was an accurate portrayal, and what did he do? He burst out laughing. I forgot to mention what a wonderful laugh he has. You have to hear it for yourself!"

She sends me Yanay's phone number, and I write it on a Post-it. I tell her that I'll call him soon, when I muster up the courage. He sounds a little *too* good to be true.

Besides, I'm exhausted. All this dating has done me in.

A few days pass. I don't call him.

Mae's leap into kindergarten is huge for both of us. I'm writing my book now. There are piles of dirty laundry on the floor. A deadline looms for an article for *Parenting* magazine on how to deal with picky eaters. I'm now running a single-parents class every Monday night in Oakland.

In short, I'm actually so busy and burned out from dating that the thought of calling a man, even one who sounds so great, is not on my top ten list—for a change.

A week and a half later, on Friday, there's another email from Dianna:

> *Rachel,*
> *Well, what happened to the courage thing?*
> *Shabbat shalom.*
>   *Dianna*

The Israeli has fallen to the curb.

Dianna's email arrives just as we're rushing out the door, on our way to Half Moon Bay for Mae's kindergarten camping trip. I promise myself that I'll call Yanay when I get home.

Sunday evening, when Mae is happily drawing a self-portrait in the kitchen, I go into the living room and dial Yanay's cell phone.

"Hello?" he answers in his thick Hebrew accent.

"Uh, hi," I say. "This is Rachel. Your friend, Dianna, sent me an email—"

"Hello!" he says again, warmly. And then he laughs. Damn, he does have the most beautiful laugh I've ever heard, full-bellied and open.

He tells me that he's driving back from Santa Cruz, where he spent the day with some kibbutznik friends who just had a baby.

"The baby is *sooooo* cute," he adds in his oh-so-sexy voice. "And what did you do this weekend?"

I tell him about our kindergarten camping trip: "I accidentally set up our tent next to some dad who snored like a bear all night."

"I don't snore," he says, and he's laughing again.

I break out into a huge smile. My body softens. I've got to sit down.

"You don't sound tough at all!" I say.

"Maybe I'm just tough around the edges," he says.

My heart is pounding. My fingertips tap on the edge of the sofa.

"Would you like to meet sometime?" Yanay asks.

A week later, I've lined my sister up for childcare. Yanay and I will meet at 3 PM at Peet's Coffee on 4ᵗʰ Street—Yanay's regular hangout—to walk around the Berkeley Marina. It was his idea to stroll around the water, and I'm so relieved. It's a beautiful, balmy day, and I can't imagine a better way to spend a first date. Forget the fancy skirt and heels. I'm wearing loose cotton pants, a T-shirt, and my worn sneakers.

A man with salt-and-pepper hair in a black leather jacket is sitting on the border of the concrete walkway in the sunshine. He stands up and opens his arms to me. His brown eyes are twinkling.

He's laughing. I'm laughing, too. Somehow, I feel right at home.

"Tell me about your daughter," Yanay says.

Ah. A good man. I pull her snapshots from my wallet.

"Oh, just look at her!" he says, taking the photos from me. "What's she like?"

"She's quite the negotiator right now," I say.

"That's my kind of girl."

I tell him about how when I left the house just twenty minutes ago she made a deal with me: "Mom, if you're going out, and I'm staying at home with Aunt Rebecca, then you need to let me have three cookies."

He tells me about the successful contracting business he has run for over a decade in the East Bay.

"I'm planning to buy a house in the next couple of years," I say.

"If you need any help looking at places, it would be my pleasure," he says.

Let's find a love shack, I think, but don't dare say out loud.

"I'm writing a book," I tell Yanay.

"What's it about?" he asks.

"My hunt for a man," I say, half-jokingly.

He stops walking. "Are you saying that I'm prey?"

We're laughing again.

When other men discover what my book is about, they get tense and anxious. One man asked if I was tape-recording our date. Another man begged me not to use his name in print.

But Yanay is light and easy. As we walk along the windy path, he tells me that he's been on JDate for over a year.

"No way!" I say. "I was on JDate, too."

"I never saw you," he says.

"I never saw you, either," I say. "But it's better this way, don't you think?"

"Yes," he agrees.

We talk about sailboats, the stalemate in the Middle East, and single motherhood. He wants to sail around the world one day. *I'll be your stowaway,* I think.

Yes, he's very opinionated about Middle Eastern politics. "It's not about oil or weapons," he tells me. "It's all about Iran. Keep your eyes on the news. You'll see."

He's a great storyteller; he enlightens me about his boyhood adventures on the kibbutz. He's also a great listener. And guess what? He *does* seem nice, in a sturdy kind of way.

He's a Man with a capital "M." He rides a motorcycle. He plays pool. He tells dirty jokes to his guy friends. He's a man, man, man—not a boy, thank God!

Our first date ends with a long hug next to his big yellow pickup truck.

"I'd like to see you again," he says.

"Me, too," I gush.

Yanay invites me out to dinner on Friday night. I take Mae to Siobhan's house for a sleepover. I've told her, "Mama is going out to dinner with a special friend." Yanay has offered to pick me up there, but Siobhan doesn't want him coming to her door. "I don't know this guy!" she says, always cautious.

So, I ask Yanay to park at the BART station two blocks from Siobhan's and call me on my cell when he gets there. Then I'll walk over to the station to meet him.

Mae and Hazel are playing dolls and Siobhan is draining a pot of pasta when my cell phone buzzes.

"Okay," I say to Yanay. "I'll walk over to BART now."

But Siobhan rushes in. "No, stop. Let him come over. I know I can be paranoid. I'll stop now."

"Are you sure?" I say.

"Yes."

When Yanay comes upstairs, he is in awe of Siobhan's apartment. Everyone is. She has a land turtle named Dottie and a cat named Pixie. She has had *many* cats in her lifetime, and she has saved all of their tiny milk teeth in a little bottle. When you look around her home, there are old bones, pieces of driftwood, and felt dolls that she sewed. Every time you turn your head, there's something new: a life-size rooster, breasts with fake fur sewn on, photos of her Grandma Frances. On her rug are strips of bright felt, buttons, and little ribbons.

Yanay finds a chair in the center of the living room, along with a pack of cards.

"Girls, come here," I yell out to Mae and Hazel.

They rush in, and I introduce Yanay.

"Hello, girls," he says in his delicious Israeli accent.

"Hi," each girl squeaks out.

"Ready for a card trick?" he says.

We all sit on our knees in front of him. It's the trick where one of the girls picks a card from the stack and shows it to the other girl—without letting him see. And then, after shuffling the cards, he magically picks out the one they'd chosen.

The first time he tries the trick, he picks the wrong card.

"No!" Mae and Hazel say.

He tries again.

"No!" they say again.

He laughs. I'm not kidding, this man has the most scrumptious laugh.

He tries the trick a third time, but still, he doesn't get it right.

"I'm rusty," he says, laughing again.

Later, Siobhan tells me that this is what she liked about Yanay: "When the card game wasn't going right, he didn't get upset. He didn't get defensive. Or mad. He just laughed. That's unusual for a man."

The first time that Yanay comes over to our apartment, I'm buzzing around the kitchen, making rice, a veggie stir-fry, and a colorful salad.

"I don't know how you do it," he says.

"Do what?" I say.

"Everything," he says. "Look at you. I haven't seen you stop."

I laugh. It's true. Single mothers don't stop.

I walk over to him and rub his shoulder. I whisper into his ear, "You know, honey, it's okay to get up and help me."

He laughs—and he does get up. He cuts the bread into little slices and pours Mae a glass of milk.

That night, Yanay shows Mae how to kill a moth on our ceiling with a slingshot he makes out of a little piece of paper and a rubber band.

Ah, this is why I need a man here.

One of his guy friends asked me recently, "Don't you think that Yanay is like the Israeli version of Kramer on *Seinfeld?*"

It's true: He's just as goofy and sincere as Kramer—but sexier and more huggable.

So far, he seems to be a good balance to my sensitive, moody side. He doesn't carry around a lot of heavy baggage or any debts. He's very close to his eighty-one-year-old mom, a Holocaust survivor, who lives in Israel.

His friend Dianna sends me another email that dissolves me: "Yanay is so excited about you! This is the first time I've heard him this enthusiastic about a relationship. (Mind you, it's in his typical tempered style.) He's more full of joy than I've ever seen."

Dear reader, I must pause here.

It's time for me to close the door on us. You can't come into my bedroom this time; it is private. I'm afraid to reveal him too quickly, too soon.

I want to tell you how he wraps his arm around me at night, all night, and how he tucks my feet in between his calves to keep them warm. I want to tell you how he swings Mae in the kitchen every night in big circles, and how I rub the patch of black hair on his chest.

We've been going out only for five months now. If you look at our relationship developmentally, we're still in the baby stage. We're barely sitting up; we're just beginning to trust.

But there's something about the way we look into each other's eyes now, and the way we touch each other. Is he my future partner? Is he the man who'll come to bed with me for the rest of my life?

It's too early to tell.

But I do know that Mae loves his paper airplanes and riding on his shoulders. When he rings our doorbell, she flies down the stairs and right into his arms. This melts me every time. We walk around the marina, the three of us, with Mae perched atop Yanay's shoulders.

Yanay meets everyone in my family: my mom and stepdad, my dad, my sister. They all like him.

"He's very smart," my dad says.

I can say undeniably, however, that *not* everything with Yanay is perfect.

He wants to have a baby.

I don't. At least not right now.

While he's tough, he's also full of estrogen—I've never heard a man long for a baby like this before. He wants his baby ASAP. It freaks me out.

"I have Mae," I tell him. "I don't want another baby. I'm done."

"You're only thirty-three," he says. "How can you be so sure?"

"I'm sure." And then I ask, "Would you consider adopting Mae?"

"Yes," he says.

The thought of having another child terrifies me. Maybe because I've never done it with a partner before. Maybe because I'm just beginning to discover who I really am and I don't want to give that up.

"I'm forty-four," he says. "I'm old."

"But you're a man," I say. "Your clock isn't ticking."

"It is," he says.

The Baby.

Every time we see each other—for coffee at Peet's or a burrito with Mae—we talk about The Baby.

I like the fact that everything is on the table. No secrets. But The Baby is our deal breaker.

Just before the New Year 2006, we are bickering about The Baby.

"It sounds like we need to break up," I say.

"It does," he says.

"I'm sad," I say.

"I'm sad, too," he says.

We hug.

I call Siobhan and Arden and cry on the phone. Both of them have already given him the thumbs-up. Both thumbs.

"He adores you," Arden says.

The ever-observant Siobhan knows this can't be the end. "More will be revealed," she tells me.

My mom calls, too: "You're making a mistake. He's a gem."

"I know, Mom."

"You know how you're always talking about all those nice Jewish dads who belong to Mae's friends?" she says.

"Yes," I say.

"Well, none of them can hold a candle to Yanay!"

"I know, Mom."

"He has the best sense of humor," she says.

"It's true."

"He seems like a rock-solid, happy human being. And he's crazy about you and Mae! Just have the baby."

"Mom!" I say, red in the face with anger. "Don't tell me what to do!"

Then Dianna sends me another email:

*I'm so sad to hear the news about you and Yanay. I heard
there were "negotiations" going on, but assumed compromises
would be made and the relationship would get stronger, not end!*

*Oh, this is just not right! You both care for each other so much,
and are so good for each other.*

In the meantime, Yanay and I keep hanging out. We like each
other. We simply like being in each other's presence. He invites me
to a friend's Chinese New Year's party in downtown Oakland.

I tell his Israeli buddies at the wine table, "You know that we
broke up, right?"

They nod their heads, looking confused. That's because we
don't look like a couple that has just broken up. We laugh. We
stand close to each other, talking. We look into each other's eyes
with longing.

Of course, at the party, I can't help but read the Chinese signs
posted on the wall. I'm a rat. He's an ox. Supposedly, rats and
oxen are very compatible.

Then Dianna invites us to San Francisco for dinner. One of
their mutual friends, Heidi, will be there. She's a local doula, and
I met her at the New Year's party; we hit it off. Of course, Mae is
invited, too. Dianna is six-months pregnant with her first child.
Nothing but babies all around.

We sit at the dining room table eating chicken and potatoes.
Mae sits in Yanay's lap. He rubs the small of her back.

"Okay, what's going on here?" Dianna asks.

"She dumped me," Yanay says.

"That's your version," I say.

"But doesn't it make you feel better?" he asks, smiling at me.

"No."

"Look," Dianna says. "I don't get it. You two are perfect for
each other."

"Perfect," Heidi agrees from across the table.

"But The Baby," I say.

She looks at Yanay. "Can you let the baby go for a couple of years?"

He nods his head.

"See how easy that was?" Dianna says to me. "He can compromise!"

"But—" I say, thinking, *Why wasn't he this easy with me?* Maybe he *is* tough around the edges.

"Just look at you!" Dianna says. "You belong together! You can't break up."

"We can't?" I say.

"No, you can't," says Heidi. "No more baby talk for a few months. Just hang out. Have fun. Don't bring the baby up again until April, okay?"

"Okay," Yanay says.

"Okay," I say.

And just like that, we're back together.

He calls me "Hot Mama."

He calls Mae "Little Shmoopy."

I tell Yanay, "You realize that Mae thinks that you're *her* boyfriend, too?"

She adores him just as much as I do.

Last Friday, Mae left for a sleepover at my mom and stepdad's. Yanay and I hung out around Berkeley, relaxing, eating dinner out. He went home on Sunday afternoon.

Then Mae came back. My stepdad brought her to the door with her suitcase. I had really missed her.

"Mae!" I said. "I missed you!"

She buzzed right past me, up the stairs.

"Honey, can't I have a hug?"

"Where's Yanay?" she said. She stomped into the living room. "Where's Yanay?"

She wanted him. Not me.

Ah. Isn't this how every single mom wishes her child would feel about her boyfriend?

As I write, Yanay is adding a second floor to his Berkeley house, two miles from me. He's been itching to do this for years; just after we met, the city approved his building plans.

When Mae and I drop by after school, he shows her how to drill screws into the wood. They hold the heavy drill together.

"It's too loud, Mommy!"

I stand behind her and cover her ears with my hands.

"Let's make a bench!" she says to Yanay.

And they do, in twenty minutes—a lovely wooden bench just for her.

"Do you notice anything new?" he asks me.

I look around. "Hey, you got a bathtub!"

"I'm a shower guy," he says. "But I know that you and Mae love baths. So I put in a super-deep bath for you two."

When I tell Yanay that I'm putting him in the book, he says just one thing: "Just make sure you tell them how good I am in bed, okay?"

Ah, men.

Tonight, I climb into Mae's bed to read her favorite book out loud, *Junie B. Jones Loves Handsome Warren.* But when the story is over, she's restless.

"I want Yanay!" she cries.

I know that she's probably just trying to use him to stay up longer. But it's hard for me to say no to this request. I call out to Yanay, who's lying on the sofa under Mae's Barbie Princess and the Pauper Slumber Bag watching CNN. He jumps up and goes right to her.

I make a beeline for the kitchen so I can pack Mae's school lunch for tomorrow.

"Rub my back," I hear her say.

"Okay, Shmoopy," he says.

Ten minutes later, I peek into the room to spy on them, and he's still standing there, in position, patting her back.

At last, she's asleep, and Yanay and I lie in my bed together, cuddling.

"I'm so lucky," I say.

"No, I'm so lucky," he says.

Someone pinch me, please.

Postscript: Where Are They Now?

ERIC

In the fall of 2005, Arden called me and said, "You're not going to believe this! You know how my sister moved to Dublin, Ireland, a few years ago?"

"Yeah," I said.

"Well, she was working at the farmer's market there when this African American guy came by who she said looked just like Mae."

Because I stayed in touch with his brother, I knew that Eric was living in Dublin. Not too many African American men around those parts. I sent an email to Arden's sister with a photo of Eric attached.

Sure enough, it was Eric.

OTIS, MY UPS MAN

About a year ago, when we were visiting New York, I knew that I wanted to see my UPS man again. After all, he was my very first crush as a single mom.

The last time I'd seen Otis three years earlier, I told him we were moving to California. He gave me a hug. I gave him a little snapshot of Mae, which he slipped into the vinyl plastic folder inside his truck. I thought that was perfect: Mae would still be smiling inside his truck, even after we were gone.

Now, I wanted to look hot. I'd lost all of my baby weight since he'd seen me last, and I could squeeze—almost—into a tight pair of pink shorts and a halter top.

"We're going to visit our old neighborhood," I told Mae, who was then five.

"Yeah!" she jumped up and down.

When we hopped on the A train and rode up to 190th Street, I silently hoped that Otis would be in the neighborhood, making deliveries, even though I knew my chances were slim. After all, it had been a long time. Surely, he'd been transferred to a new route by now, or he'd been given an office job because of his injured knee.

When Mae and I got off the train, there was no UPS truck in sight. We walked over to the playground, where I told Mae about the first time she went down a slide by herself, right here. The same ice cream man was still there in his ice cream truck, and we bought Popsicles from him.

Just when I'd licked my Popsicle down to the stick, there it was: the big brown truck.

"Mae!" I said. "It's the UPS truck!"

She looked at me with scrunched-up eyebrows. "So?"

"C'mon, Mae," I said, pulling on her arm. "We've got to see if Otis is there."

We crossed the street. But she was in no hurry. "I have to use the bathroom," she said.

"This will only take a minute."

But the UPS truck was locked. No one was inside. We walked to the nearest apartment building, and sure enough, there he was, in the lobby. I knocked on the glass. He turned his head. I waved. He squinted. And then he smiled. His hand dropped from the cart, and he came right to the door, pushing it open. He wrapped his arms around me.

"Rachel!"

"Otis!"

"What are you doing here?" he asked.

"Looking for you," I said.

He looked down. "Mae! You're a girl now!"

"Do you remember Otis?" I said.

"No," she said.

"I still have your picture in my truck," he said to Mae. And then he turned to me: "You look great!"

"Thanks."

"How long are you here for?" he said.

"A week," I said. "Do you think you might get some time off?"

His eyes darted from me to the sidewalk. He suddenly seemed uncomfortable.

"You have a girlfriend now, don't you?"

He laughed, and so did I.

"Oh, Otis," I said. "My new UPS man in California is nerdy. I miss you."

Otis will always be my special delivery—if only in my fantasies.

RAUL, OUR BUILDING MANAGER

The same summer I tracked down Otis, I called Raul. I wanted to thank him. For being the first person to call us after the World Trade towers went down. For being the first man not related to us to step into our lives and care about us. Yes, he was one of the first men to become part of our platonic, loving male tribe.

One hot afternoon, he met us at a Midtown playground, where Mae ran through the sprinklers in her bikini. She was barefoot and shrieking with happiness. Her hair was soaking wet.

"Just look at her," Raul said, shaking his head. "She's all grown up."

Mae rushed by and sprinkled Raul's face with water. That was her way of saying, "I remember you!"

VICTOR, BOYFRIEND NO. 1

I wish there was some way I could thank Victor, truly thank him, for my first courageous plunge into the dating world as a single mom.

We've stayed in touch over the past few years: sporadic, heartfelt phone calls and handmade cards sent on special occasions. He remembers Mae's birthday every year, and has sent her care packages: a sequined cowgirl dress, a plastic dinosaur, a cup in the shape of a cat. This year, he mailed a book of games that can be done with a string, such as cat's cradle. When I show Mae photos of Victor, she smiles, making me believe she remembers him. He even visited us once when he was in the Bay Area for a statistics conference. But I'd just started dating someone new, and it was awkward, both of us sleeping side-by-side on my sofa bed, in all our clothes, our bodies tight with sexual tension.

Last fall, while having a drink at a bar with writer-friends, I went outside and called Victor from my cell phone.

"Hi!" I said. "What are you up to?"

"Rachel!" he said. "It's great to hear from you."

"Oh, Victor!" I said.

"Excuse me?"

"Shit," I cursed under my breath.

I'd just called him by the name I'd given him in this book.

"What did you just call me?" he said.

JIM, WHO CAME QUICKLY

In 2005, two years after our breakup, I saw Jim's name in my inbox. My first thought was, "Oh, damn, he found out that I'm writing about our sex life!"

Hi. How are you? I hope all is well. I have been thinking about you a lot lately for lots of different reasons and thought I'd shoot you this email. I spent a large part of today just sitting in the sun and reflecting and it was nice.

Anyway, just wanted you to know that I think about you and Mae often.

Sounds like a booty call. But at least I hadn't been caught. Yet.

TOM, THE FISH MAN

I'd just put down the last lines on this very postscript when I ran out the door to return a kid's video that was two weeks late—we'd left it at my stepfather's house—before picking up Mae.

I was thinking about the fact that I'd skipped over many men here, simply because I never saw them again. Tom, the fish man, was one of these guys. I hadn't seen him for three years.

That very day, I was hustling down the sidewalk when I heard "Rachel!" I turned my head. A deep male voice was coming from a blue sports car I didn't recognize. The car stopped on the corner.

Uh-oh. A tall, muscular African American man was walking toward me, smiling. He waved.

Tom?

"How are you?" he said. "How's Mae?"

Of course, the first thing I did was find Mae's kindergarten photo in my wallet and show it to him.

"Beautiful!" he says. And she is.

"You know what's really funny?" he said, laughing. "I've been thinking about you!"

I laughed, too. Because, boy-oh-boy, had I been thinking about him. And writing about him.

"It's good to see you," he said. "I'd love to talk to you some more."

I told him that I was seeing someone now—but that it was nice to see him. And it was.

MY DAD

There's no doubt about it: Mae adores her grandpa. Mae, who will turn six in a couple of weeks, now leaves messages on her grandpa's voice mail, such as "Will you please take me to a movie?" Mondays are still their special days.

This weekend, her photo is on the front page of the *San Francisco Chronicle Datebook*. It was taken when she and her grandpa recently visited the local kids' museum. Those two sure get around.

The adoration is mutual. My dad wrote this in a recent email to Mae:

> *You make my heart buzz.*
> *Want to see* Curious George *next week? I love you.*
> > *Always yours,*
> > *Grandpa*

As for my dad and me, we're still working out our boundaries. Sometimes, when he tells me how to lead my life, I want to yell, "Time out, Dad!" But I dread losing yet another important man in our lives.

Despite my dad's faults and the complications of our relationship, Mae and I need and love him. That's enough—at this moment.

YANAY

In the spring of 2006, Yanay, Mae, and I are at Crepevine on College Avenue. I'm the only one actually eating a crepe. Yanay has a pancake, and Mae has a cookie.

After pouring syrup on top of his pancake, Yanay looks up and says, "Why don't you two move in with me?"

"Excuse me?" I say, almost choking.

"We could try it," he says. "Just take this step and see how it goes."

There's a big piece of mushroom crepe in my mouth. He's caught me off guard. I turn red.

"You're blushing," he says. "Look at you!"

I stop chewing. "Did you just say, 'Move in with you'?"

He nods.

"Uh, I don't know," I say.

"I'm offering you what I have," he says. "The second floor is done. I'm not sure where Mae's room will go, but we can figure that out."

I put my fork down. Is he serious?

He's still talking. "I'll ask you to cover half of the monthly mortgage," he says. "But that will be a lot less than what you're paying now."

But I'm still thinking about how we'll fit into his life. Or, how he'll fit into ours.

"Can we get a kitten?" I ask. I don't know why I say this, it's the first thing that comes to my mind.

"A kitty!" screams Mae, who has been eavesdropping all this time.

"And a dog," Yanay says.

That's when my eyes fill with tears.

"Oh no, sweetie," he says. "Are you crying? What's wrong?"

"Nothing," I sniffle. "Everything is just right."

Acknowledgments

Siobhan Van Winkel, thank you for "Don't go back for more where there is only less."

Arden Fredman, thank you for "Every woman must have a first-date skirt."

Hazel and Celia, I love you, too.

Thank you Dad, Mom, Bill, and Rebecca.

Amanda Riesman, my sensible soul mate.

My writing group, for the magic . . . you know what I'm talking about . . . Annie Kassof, Kathy Briccetti, Lynn Goodwin, Suzanne LaFetra, Ronnie Chater, Sybil Lockhart.

Jill Rothenberg, much more than an editor, dating-comrade-in-arms, who told me, "Your sex scenes move too fast."

Editor and sister-friend extraordinaire, Laura Mazer.

Fellow Naughty Mommy, Heidi Raykeil.

Tabitha Lahr, for putting me in heels on the cover.

Rose Carrano, for jumping on board as a super-publicist.

My comrades-on-the-page . . . columnists and editors at *Literary Mama*.

My agent, Becky Kurson, who hung in there with me for the long haul.

Waleska and Valeria Herrera, *Gracias, mis amores.*

Amy and Elyza Pogrebin, Mexico, here we come . . .

All the families at the BRJCC who took care of my daughter when I had a date!

Patricia Codrington, for helping me back on my feet.

Premsiri Lewin, for holding my hand when I needed it.

David Steele, for showing me how to date consciously.

In loving memory of Norine Smith, my single mom hero who left us too suddenly.

Hunter Mann, the godfather.

Ralph Manak and Eric Reynolds, stylish Web-men and great guys.

Susan Light and Jim Rogers, for setting me up on my first blind date.

V., No. 1 Boyfriend.

Yanay Shik, for taking on not one but two feisty females.

About the Author

Rachel Sarah's column on single motherhood and dating, "Single Mom Seeking," appears in the web magazine *Literary Mama*.

Currently, she is the dating and romance columnist for *J.*, the Jewish newsweekly of Northern California, for which the American Jewish Press Association awarded her a Simon Rockower 2005 Award for Excellence in Jewish Journalism. She has written for *Elle, Parenting, Ms., Family Circle, Pregnancy, Washington Post, San Francisco Examiner,* and *Tango.*

Sarah leads workshops for singles and lives in the San Francisco Bay Area with her daughter.

You can reach her at www.singlemomseeking.com.

© JOHANNAH HETHERINGTON

Selected Titles from Seal Press

For more than thirty years, Seal Press has published groundbreaking books. By women. For women. Visit our website at www.sealpress.com.

Confessions of a Naughty Mommy: How I Found My Lost Libido by Heidi Raykeil. $14.95. 1-58005-157-X. The Naughty Mommy shares her bedroom woes and woo-hoos with other mamas who are rediscovering their sex lives after baby and are ready to think about it, talk about it, and DO it.

The Truth Behind the Mommy Wars: Who Decides What Makes a Good Mother? by Miriam Peskowitz. $15.95. 1-58005-129-4. A groundbreaking book that reveals the truth behind the "wars" between working mothers and stay-at-home moms.

Dirty Sugar Cookies: Culinary Observations, Questionable Taste by Ayun Halliday. $14.95, 1-58005-150-2. Ayun Halliday is back with comical and unpredictable essays about her disastrous track record in the kitchen and her culinary observations—though she's clearly no expert.

I Wanna Be Sedated: 30 Writers on Parenting Teenagers edited by Faith Conlon and Gail Hudson. $15.95. 1-58005-127-8. With hilarious and heartfelt essays, this anthology will reassure any parent of a teenager that they are not alone in their desire to be comatose.

It's a Boy: Women Writers on Raising Sons by Andrea J. Buchanan. $14.95, 1-58005-145-6. Seal's edgy take on what it's really like to raise boys, from toddlers to teens and beyond.

Woman's Best Friend: Women Writers on the Dogs in Their Lives edited by Megan McMorris. $14.95, 1-58005-163-4. An offbeat and poignant collection about those four legged friends girls can't do without.